好一朵茉莉花

What a Beautiful Jasmine Flower

3B

顾　问：魏崇新　张晓慧　吴丽君
主　编：朱　勇
编　著：池　宇
翻　译：李娟娟

外语教学与研究出版社
FOREIGN LANGUAGE TEACHING AND RESEARCH PRESS
北京 BEIJING

图书在版编目（CIP）数据

好一朵茉莉花＝What a Beautiful Jasmine Flower：3B/池宇编著；李娟娟译．－北京：外语教学与研究出版社，2009.3（2011.6重印）
(外研社汉语分级读物：中文天天读／朱勇主编)
ISBN 978－7－5600－8237－0

Ⅰ.好… Ⅱ.①池… ②李… Ⅲ.汉语—对外汉语教学－语言读物 Ⅳ.H195.5

中国版本图书馆CIP数据核字（2009）第034388号

出 版 人：于春迟
责任编辑：颜丽娜
装帧设计：姚　军
插图绘制：北京碧悠动漫文化有限公司
出版发行：外语教学与研究出版社
社　　址：北京市西三环北路19号（100089）
网　　址：http://www.fltrp.com
印　　刷：北京盛通印刷股份有限公司
开　　本：889×1194　1／16
印　　张：7
版　　次：2009年3月第1版 2011年6月第2次印刷
书　　号：ISBN 978－7－5600－8237－0
定　　价：39.00元（含CD光盘一张）
*　　*　　*

物料号：182370001

编写说明

众所周知，阅读是成人外语学习者获得语言输入的重要方式。只有加强阅读，增加语言输入量，才能更快地学好一门外语。基于此，如何让学习者有效利用课余时间，通过快乐阅读、随意阅读来促进其语言学习，一直是众多语言教学与研究者所关注的课题之一。

令人遗憾的是，适合各种水平汉语学习者阅读需要的汉语分级读物，长期以来一直处于相对短缺的状态。鉴于此，外语教学与研究出版社2007年发起并组织编写了本套系列汉语分级读物——《中文天天读》，用于满足各级水平汉语学习者的阅读需求，让学习者在快乐阅读的同时有效提高自己的汉语水平。同时，也通过巧妙的关于中国社会、历史、文化背景的介绍与传达，为所有汉语学习者真正开启一扇了解当代中国的窗口。

《中文天天读》按语言难度分为5级，每级各有A、B、C等不同的分册，可适合不同级别的学习者使用。文章字数等具体说明请看下表。

级　别	文章字数	词汇量	篇　目	已学时间
1级	100～150	500	25篇	三个月（160学时）
2级	150～300	1000	25篇	半年（320学时）
3级	300～550	2000	25篇	一年（640学时）
4级	500～750	3500	20篇	两年（1280学时）
5级	700～1200	5000	18篇	三年（1920学时）

为方便更多语种的学习者学习，《中文天天读》将陆续出版英、日、韩、西、德、法、意、俄等十多种语言的版本，学习者可根据情况自选。

《中文天天读》大致有以下几个模块：

1. 阅读前模块——导读。导读主要是一两个跟文章有关的问题，类似于课堂导入，主要是激发学生的兴趣，起到热身的作用。

2. 阅读中模块，包括正文、边注、插图。边注是对生词进行随文对译和解释的一种方式，目的是帮助学习者扫清生词障碍，迅速获得词义。它有助于降低文章难度，保持阅读速度。插图也是《中文天天读》的一大特色。插图中反映的都是课文的核心内容，也经常出现课文中的关键句子。这些都有助于读者“见图知义”，快速理解课文内容。

3. 阅读后模块，包括语言点、练习和小知识。语言点是对重点词语或结构的简单说明。每个语言点的第一个例句大多是课文中的原句，其他例句的目的是帮助学生“温故而知新”，句子中着力使用已学课文中的生词或者语境。练习题的题型主要有问答题、选择题、判断题、填表题等，都和内容理解有关。《中文天天读》的题量不大，因为过多的练习会破坏阅读的乐趣。小知识中，有的是跟文章内容密切相关的背景知识，读了以后直接有助于理解课文；有的跟文章有一定关系，是对课文内容的补充和延伸；还有一种则属于一般性的中国文化、历史地理知识介绍。

与同类材料相比，《中文天天读》具有以下特点：

1. 易读易懂。“容易些，再容易些”是我们编写《中文天天读》一直持有的理念。对于每篇选文的生词、字数我们都有严格的控制。我们还通过为边注词、小知识等配以英、日、韩、西等不同语种译文的方式，方便学习者更好地理解课文。此外，每课均配有与课文、小知识内容匹配的漫画或图片，通过这些关键线索，唤起读者大脑中的相关图式，有效地起到助读的作用。

2. 多样有趣。“兴趣是最好的老师”，我们力求选文富有情趣。选文伊始，我们即根据已有经验以及相关调查，对留学生的需求进行了分析，尽可能保证选文在一定程度上能够投其所好。具体做法是：(1) 话题多样，内容丰富。这样可以保持阅读的新鲜感。《中文天天读》各册从普通中国人的衣食住行、传统风俗与现代生活的交替到中国当代的社会、经济、语言、文化等内容均有涉及，有的还从中外对比的角度来叙述和分析，力求让读者了解到中国社会的真实面貌，同时还可以对学生的跨文化交际能力起到一定的指导作用；（2）文体多样，形式活泼。《中文天天读》中，记叙文、说明文、议论文、书信、诗歌、小小说等文体不拘一格，让读者充分了解汉语的不同体裁，感受中文的魅力。

3. 注重实用。选文比较实用，其中不少文章都贴近留学生的生活。有的文章本身就是一些有助于留学生在中国的学习、生活、旅行、工作的相关介绍，可以学以致用。

4. 听读结合。《中文天天读》每册均配有相应的CD或MP3，读者既可以通过“读”的方式欣赏地道的中文，也可以通过“听”的方式感受纯正的普通话。这两种输入方式会从不同的角度帮助学习者提高汉语水平。

在编写过程中，我们从阅读教学专家、全国对外汉语优秀教师刘颂浩先生那里获益良多；我的同事马晓冬博士提出了许多建设性的意见；外语教学与研究出版社汉语分社给予该项目以大力支持，李彩霞、李扬、庄晶晶、颜莉、于辉、许杨等编辑为《中文天天读》的策划、编写做出了特别贡献；北外中文学院2006级、2007级的10多位研究生在项目启动之初的选文方面也给我们很多帮助，在此一并致谢！

欢迎广大同行、读者批评指导，也欢迎大家将使用过程中发现的问题反馈给我们，以便再版时更上一层楼。联系方式：zhuyong1706@gmail.com。

朱勇
2011年5月

Preface

It is common knowledge that reading is an important input channel for adult learners of a foreign language. Extensive reading can ensure adequate language input and fast, efficient learning. Therefore, both language researchers and teachers emphasize large amount of reading in addition to classroom learning.

Regrettably, well designed and appropriately graded reading materials for second-language learners are hard to come by. Aware of the shortage, the Foreign Language Teaching and Research Press initiated in 2007 the compilation of *Reading China*, a series of readers tailored to the diverse needs of learners at different levels of Chinese proficiency. The readers feature fun stories of present-day China, with introductions on Chinese history, culture and everyday life.

There are altogether five levels in the series, each consisting of several volumes. Please refer to the table below for specific data:

Level	Length of Texts (words)	Vocabulary	Number of Texts	Prior Chinese Learning
1	100 ～ 150	500	25	Three months (160 credit hours)
2	150 ～ 300	1000	25	Half a year (320 credit hours)
3	300 ～ 550	2000	25	One year (640 credit hours)
4	500 ～ 750	3500	20	Two years (1280 credit hours)
5	700 ～ 1200	5000	18	Three years (1920 credit hours)

Other language versions of the series, such as Japanese, Korean, Spanish, German, French, Italian and Russian, will come off the press soon to facilitate the study of Chinese learners with these language backgrounds.

Each book of the series includes the following modules:

1. Pre-reading—Lead-in. This part has one or two interesting warming-up questions, which function as an introduction to a new text.

2. Reading—Texts, Side Notes and Illustrations. Side Notes provide equivalents and explanations for new words and expressions to help learners better understand the text. This part also keeps the degree of difficulty of the texts within reasonable bounds so that learners can read them at a reasonable speed. Illustrations are another highlight of the series. They help learners take in at a glance the key sentences and main ideas of the texts.

3. After-reading—Language Points, Exercises and Cultural Tips. The Language Points part hammers home the meaning and usage of important words and expressions, or grammar points in one of the sentences from the text. Two follow-up example sentences, usually with words, expressions or linguistic contexts from previous texts, are given to help learners "gain new insights through review of old materials". In Exercises, a small amount of questions, choice questions, true or false questions and cloze tests, are designed to check learners' comprehension of the texts without spoiling the fun of reading. In Cultural Tips, background information is provided as supplementary reading materials. Some are related to the texts and some are just general information about Chinese culture, history and geography.

Reading China stands out among similar readers because of the following features:

1. User-friendliness: "Reading should be as easy as possible", a principle consistently followed by the compilers, through strict control of the number of new words and expressions in each text, the Side Notes, the translations given in Language Points and Cultural Tips, illustrations and pictures.

2. Diversity and fun: The compilers have taken great pains in choosing interesting stories because "interest is the best teacher". We also try to cater to foreign students' reading preferences by analyzing their learning expectations on the basis of our teaching experience and surveys. Firstly, a wide range of topics is included to sustain the freshness of reading. The stories touch upon many aspects of Chinese life. In some cases, similarities and differences between Chinese and foreign cultures are compared and analyzed to give learners a realistic idea about contemporary China and improve their cross-cultural communication ability. Secondly, different writing genres and styles are selected, such as narrations, instructions, argumentations, letters, poems, mini-stories, etc. In this way, learners can fully appreciate the charm of the Chinese language.

3. Practicality: Many texts are closely related to foreign students' life in China and contain practical information about studying, living, traveling and working in China.

4. Listening materials: MP3 or CDs are provided for each book of the series. Integration of audio input through listening and visual input through reading will further improve learning results.

In the course of our compilation work, we have benefited a great deal from the expertise of Mr. Liu Songhao, an expert in teaching Chinese reading and an excellent teacher of Chinese as a second language. Dr. Ma Xiaodong, my colleague, has provided many inspiring suggestions. Our heartfelt gratitude goes to the directors and editors of the FLTRP Chinese Publishing Division, in particular Li Caixia, Li Yang, Zhuang Jingjing, Yan Li, Yu Hui and Xu Yang, for their contribution to the planning and compilation of this series. We also wish to thank more than ten postgraduate students of the years 2006 and 2007 at BFSU for their help in collecting materials at the early stage of this project.

We would greatly appreciate suggestions and comments from learners and teachers of Chinese as a second language and would accordingly improve the books in the future. Contact information: zhuyong1706@gmail.com.

Zhu Yong

May, 2011

使用建议

感谢您关注并选用《中文天天读》！关于怎样更好地使用这套阅读资源，作为编者，我们在这里提出几点建议，供您参考。

一、教材选用

《中文天天读》是一套以“在快乐阅读中体验汉语并了解中国”为目的的分级读物。因为它每一册的容量都不太大，每一课都编配有语言点例释和练习，所以又可以作为专门的阅读教材来使用。

教师可以根据《中文天天读》“编写说明”中每一级在长度、词汇量、篇目等方面的信息，结合学习者的水平来选用相应级别的教材。《中文天天读》每一级又包括A、B、C3册，其难度为A<B≤C，每一册的容量减少，使其适合国外的学时。这样国外选用时从3册中选取1册或2册，国内选用时根据学时选用2册或3册。教师可按照先A后B再C的顺序展开教学。如果是习惯给学生留课外作业的老师，也可以把相应级别中较为容易的A册或B册作为课外阅读任务，让学生课下完成，相应地，以B册或C册作为课堂教学的教材。

二、课程进度

《中文天天读》纸质版本中每课的练习量都比较少，一般来说，2课时左右可以完成1–2篇课文的教学。如果是国内的长期教学，每周2–4课时的话，一学期可以完成两册书的教学。如果是短期教学或者在国外课时比较少的情况下，一个教学周期一般能完成一册书的教学。另外，我们设立了《中文天天读》配套网络资源库（博客“大家的《中文天天读》”http://blog.sina.com.cn/u/1869145497），逐步将每一课的补充练习置入资源库中，免费提供给所有使用者。这些练习可以作为课堂练习使用，也可以作为课后作业留给学生，但老师都要根据学生的实际情况给予必要的引导。教师也可以把课本中的练习和补充练习综合起来，自己决定课堂练习和课后作业的分配。当然，这些不同的安排可能都会影响到您具体的进度，相信每一位老师都会有比较恰当的把握。

三、教学过程

阅读前。《中文天天读》每一课的“导读”可以作为教师的导入语来使用，教师根据实际情况可以让学生进行简单的讨论；正文的插图也可以作为导入材料，让学生读前先看插图，通过插图来猜测课文反映的内容，这样课本就变成了一份看图说话的练习资料；教师也可以从听入手，在读前让学生听一遍配套的CD或MP3。这样多种途径结合，可以充分调动学习者的阅读兴趣和相关的图式背景，为更好地理解阅读材料服务。

阅读中。可以综合运用默读、轮读、小组读、带着问题查读等多种形式，使学习者对阅读材料达到充分的感知。

阅读后。《中文天天读》的练习大致可以分为四种：课文理解题主要检测学习者对课文的理解程度；语言练习题、阅读技能训练题和写作题则可以帮助学习者积累语言知识，并提高读写技能。书中的小知识可以作为课堂阅读的补充，也可以作为课下阅读材料使用，教师可在其基础上适当作一些话题扩展，将语言学习与文化习得有机结合起来，让学生在不知不觉中伴随性地获得有关中国历史文化的知识。配套的CD或MP3也可以放在读后来听，以达到复习巩固的目的。

How to Use *Reading China*

Welcome to use *Reading China*! As the compiler, we would like to offer some suggestions concerning how to better make use of this set of reading materials.

1. How to choose books

Reading China is a set of graded reading materials targeting at "experiencing Chinese and understanding China through happy reading". Since the number of lessons in each book is not too much and each lesson is equipped with Language Points and Exercises, this series can be used as reading textbooks in class.

Teachers are advised to read the "Preface" at the beginning of the books for information on length of texts, vocabulary, and number of texts of each level of books, and choose the appropriate level for the learners. There are three volumes in each level of *Reading China* – A, B and C, and the level of difficulty is A<B⩽C. The number of texts in each book is cut down so as to tally with class hours in overseas schools. Teachers using this set of books overseas can choose one or two books from a level for classroom use and teachers using the books in China can choose two or three books from a level. They can follow the order starting from Book A to Book B and then to Book C. Or, for teachers who would like to assign homework for students, they can designate Book A or Book B, which are relatively easier, as reading materials outside class and use Book B or Book C as textbooks for classroom teaching.

2. How to make the schedule

The exercises for each lesson in *Reading China* are not too much. Generally speaking, one to two texts can be finished in a two-hour class. For long-term training programs in China, two books can be covered in a semester if there are two to four class hours in a week; for short-term training programs or overseas programs, one book can be covered in a teaching session. What's more, we have established a supportive online resource pool for the series (blog: "Everyone's *Reading China*", http://blog.sina.com.cn/u/1869145497) . Supplementary exercises for each lesson will be available at the resource pool for free. These exercises can be used either as classroom exercises or as afterschool homework. In either case, teachers are advised to provide necessary guidance in accordance with students' ability. The teachers can also combine the exercises in the books and supplementary exercises online and decide which ones are done in class and which are for homework. Since different arrangements may take some extra time, teachers are free to make their own schedule.

3. How to teach with this series

Pre-reading: Teachers can develop their own class introductions on the basis of Lead-in at the beginning of each lesson and think of some topics for discussions for students. On the one hand, with the help of Illustrations, students can look at the pictures before reading the texts to guess what the text is about. In this way, the series become exercise materials for "look and say" practices. On the other hand, with the help of CD or MP3, students can listen to the recording before reading the texts to get a general idea. A combination of different methods can effectively activate learners' interest in reading and enhance their knowledge of the background, so as to better help with their understanding of the texts.

Reading: There are a variety of ways of reading the texts, such as silent reading, reading in pairs, reading in groups, reading with questions in mind, through which learners can acquire an adequate perception of the reading materials.

After-reading: There are four types of exercises in *Reading China*. Apprehension questions examine learners' understanding of the texts. Language practice, reading skill trainings and writing tasks help learners accumulate knowledge about the language and improve their skill of reading and writing. Cultural Tips can serve as the extension of in-class reading or as after school reading materials. Teachers may further explore the topics to integrate language learning with cultural acquisition, so that students can acquire more knowledge about China's history and culture in an easy and interesting way. Students can listen to CD or MP3 after reading the texts to consolidate what has been learned.

目 录
Contents

1 Zuì hǎo de jiàoyù
最好的教育
The Best Education

你觉得你在什么地方学到的东西最重要？
来听听诺贝尔奖获得者的想法吧。

诺贝尔奖 (Nuòbèi'ěr Jiǎng) *n.* the Nobel prize

获得者 (huòdézhě) *n.* winner

聚会 (jùhuì) *v.* gather, get together

有一年，75 位诺贝尔奖获得者在巴黎聚会。有个记者问其中的一位："在您的一生中，您认为最重要的东西是在哪所学校学到的呢？"

这位满头白发的诺贝尔奖获得者平静地回答："是在幼儿园。"

记者感到非常惊奇，又问："为什么是在幼儿园呢？您认为您在幼儿园里学到了什么呢？"

老人微笑着回答："在幼儿园里，我学到了很多很多。比如，把自己的东西分一半给小朋友们；不是自己的东西不要拿；东西要放整齐；饭前要洗手；午饭后要休息；做了错事要道歉；学习时要多思考。我认为，我学到的全部东西就是这些。"

老人一讲完，所有的人都站起来鼓掌。事实上，大多数科学家都认为，他们一生中学到的最重要的东西，就是幼儿园老师教给他们的好习惯。

记者 (jìzhě) *n.* journalist

平静 (píngjìng) *adj.* calm, quiet

幼儿园 (yòu'éryuán) *n.* kindergarten

惊奇 (jīngqí) *adj.* amazed, surprised

道歉 (dàoqiàn) *v.* apologize

思考 (sīkǎo) *v.* think deeply

鼓掌 (gǔzhǎng) *v.* applaud

科学家 (kēxuéjiā) *n.* scientist

想一想 Questions

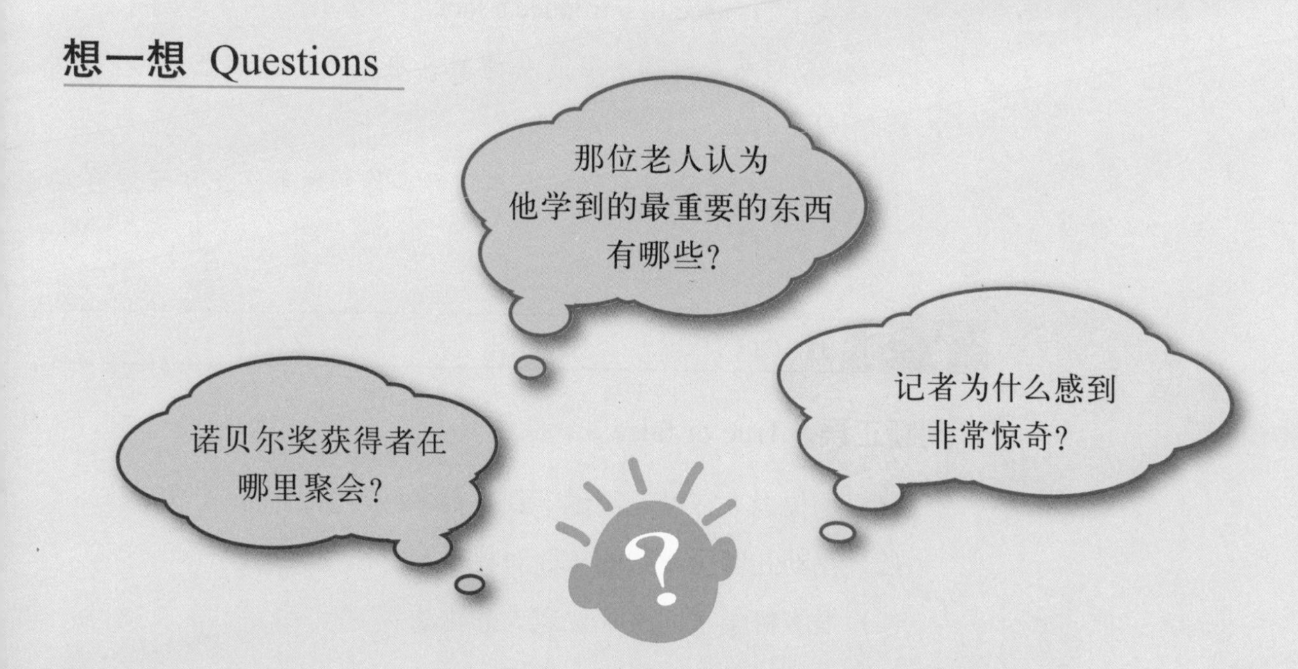

语言点 Language Points

感到
feel

1. 记者感到非常惊奇。

The journalist felt surprised.

“感到”，动词。“觉得”的意思。

“感到” is a verb which means “feel”.

(1) 昨天太累了，今天早上我感到有些不舒服。

(2) 老师说我的发音越来越好，我感到非常高兴。

事实上
in fact

2. 事实上，大多数科学家认为，他们一生中学到的最重要的东西，就是幼儿园老师教给他们的好习惯。

In fact, most scientists believe that the most important things they have learnt in life are the good habits taught by their kindergarten teachers.

“事实上”，用来介绍一个真实的情况。

“事实上” is used to introduce a fact.

(1) 人们总是觉得有钱人很幸福，事实上，他们也常有不快乐的时候。

(2) 很多人觉得学习好就能找到好工作，但事实上不是这样。

练习 Exercises

1. 判断正误。True or false.

(1) 那位老人在幼儿园里学到了很多好习惯。 (　　)

(2) 在幼儿园里学到的东西对科学家有很大帮助。 (　　)

(3) 很多科学家同意那位老人的想法。 (　　)

2. **选择正确答案。**Choose the correct answer.

（1）诺贝尔奖获得者认为最重要的东西是在（　　）学到的。

A. 大学　　B. 中学　　C. 小学　　D. 幼儿园

（2）听了老人的回答，记者觉得很（　　）。

A. 高兴　　B. 生气　　C. 伤心　　D. 吃惊

（3）（　　）不是在幼儿园学到的。

A. 把自己的东西分给朋友　　B. 饭前要洗手

C. 喜欢使用别人的东西　　D. 做了错事要道歉

小知识 Cultural Tips

诺贝尔奖
The Nobel Prize

诺贝尔奖是以瑞典著名化学家、工业家、硝化甘油炸药发明人艾尔弗雷德·伯恩哈德·诺贝尔(1833—1896年)的部分遗产作为基金创立的，它是世界上最为重要的科学奖项之一。

诺贝尔奖最初设有物理、化学、生理或医学、文学及和平五个奖项，后又增设经济学等奖项。

The Nobel prize, one of the world's most important prizes in science, was founded in part by the legacy of Alfred Bernhard Nobel (1833—1896), the famous Swedish chemist, industrialist, and inventor of nitroglycerine. Initially, there were only awards for achievements in physics, chemistry, physiology or medicine, literature and peace. Later, prizes for other subjects, like economics, were added.

2 Běijīng de sìhéyuàn 北京的四合院

Beijing's Siheyuan

你去过北京的四合院吗？
如果有机会，你一定要去看看。

建筑 (jiànzhù) *n.* architecture

元朝 (yuáncháo) *n.* Yuan Dynasty

构成 (gòuchéng) *n.* form

四合院是老北京人居住的主要建筑，在国内外都很有名。

北京四合院为什么有名呢？首先是因为它有六百多年的历史。从元朝开始，四合院就出现了。其次是它的构成非常特别，在中国传统住宅建筑中很有代表性。四合院的"四"是"东南西北"四面的意思，"合"是围在一起的意思。也就是说，四合院是由四面的房屋或院墙围成的。只要关上大门，四合院就和外面隔开了。

几百年来，北京人就在这样的四合院中生活。过去，一个四合院只住一家人。后来，一座四合院住进了两家、三家……有的四合院甚至住了十几家人，成为了现在北京人所说的“大杂院儿”。大杂院儿里邻居的亲密关系是许多老北京人永远无法忘记的。

四合院之所以有名，还因为它虽然是居住建筑，但是却有着很深的中国传统文化。目前，典型的四合院越来越少。为了让这种具有中国特色的民族建筑保存下来，北京已经开始保护四合院了。

住宅 (zhùzhái) *n.*
house, residence

代表性 (dàibiǎoxìng) *n.*
representativeness

围 (wéi) *v.*
enclose, surround

隔 (gé) *v.*
seperate, cut off

大杂院儿 (dàzáyuànr) *n.*
multi-household compound

亲密 (qīnmì) *adj.*
intimate

典型(diǎnxíng) *adj.*
typical

特色 (tèsè) *n.*
characteristics, feature

保存 (bǎocún) *v.*
preserve

想一想 Questions

语言点 Language Points

所说的
(so) called

1. **有的四合院甚至住了十几家人，成为了现在北京人所说的"大杂院儿"。**

Some *siheyuans* (quadrangles) accommodate tens of households, thus becoming what the Beijing people now call "multi-household compound".

"所"，助词。用在及物动词之前，使"所＋动词＋的"成为名词性短语。多用于书面语。

"所" is an auxiliary word, used before transitive verbs to turn the "所+ v." structures into noun phrases. It is mostly used in formal language.

(1) 大家所提的意见，我会认真考虑的。
(2) 关于这件事情，我所知道的已经都告诉你了。

无法
cannot

2. **大杂院儿里邻居的亲密关系是许多老北京人永远无法忘记的。**

The intimate relationships among the residents of the multi-household compounds of old Beijing are what they cannot ever forget.

"无法"，动词。后面常接动词。表示"不能做"或者"没有办法做"。

"无法", verb, is often followed by another verb, indicating "can not do something" or "have no way to do something".

(1) 晚上 11 点半了，还有人在唱歌，吵得他无法睡觉。
(2) 我忘了她的电话号码，所以现在无法跟她联系。

练习 Exercises

1. **判断正误。** True or false.

(1) 几百年以前，一个四合院里一般住很多家庭。 (　　)
(2) "大杂院儿"就是很多家庭住在同一个四合院里。 (　　)
(3) 北京人很喜欢大杂院儿里邻居的关系。 (　　)
(4) 北京现在还没有开始保护四合院。 (　　)

2. 选择正确答案。Choose the correct answer.

（1）北京四合院有名不是因为（　　）。

A. 四合院有很长时间的历史　　B. 四合院有很深的传统文化

C. 北京人都住在四合院里　　D. 四合院是很特别的传统建筑

（2）以下说法错误的是（　　）。

A. 早在元朝就有四合院了　　B. “四合院”中的“四”指“东西南北”

C. 大杂院儿里的人们关系很好　　D. 现在的北京，典型的四合院越来越多

小知识 Cultural Tips

四合院与胡同
Siheyuan and Hutong

胡同是北京建筑的一大特色。据研究，“胡同”这个词的发音来自蒙古语，是“水井”的意思。胡同和四合院是一体的，胡同两边是若干四合院。胡同和四合院是北京市民传统的居住方式。胡同文化是北京文化的重要组成部分。如今，北京的四合院和胡同也是来京旅游必不可少的参观项目。

Hutongs are a distinguishing architecture in Beijing. According to research, the pronunciation of the word “*hutong*” originated from Mongolian, meaning “water well”. The *hutong* and the *siheyuan* cannot be separated from each other, since the two sides of a *hutong* are walled by several *siheyuans*. *Hutongs* and *siheyuans* together represent a traditional form of local residence. The culture of *hutongs* is an important part of Beijing culture. Nowadays, the *siheyuans* and the *hutongs* are a must-see for visitors to Beijing.

3 Hǎo yì duǒ mòlìhuā
好一朵茉莉花

What a Beautiful Jasmine Flower

现在，很多外国朋友都知道《茉莉花》这首中国歌曲。
我们一起来听听吧。

茉莉花 (mòlìhuā) *n.*
jasmine flower

笑话 (xiàohua) *v.*
laugh at, ridicule

发芽 (fāyá) *v.*
sprout, burgeon

好一朵茉莉花，好一朵茉莉花，
满园花草，香也香不过它。
我有心采一朵戴，
看花的人儿要将我骂。

好一朵茉莉花，好一朵茉莉花，

茉莉花开，雪也白不过它。

我有心采一朵戴，

又怕旁人笑话。

好一朵茉莉花，好一朵茉莉花，

满园花开，比也比不过它。

我有心采一朵戴，

又怕来年不发芽。

《茉莉花》是中国最有名的民歌之一。这首民歌通过赞美茉莉花，来表现男女之间纯洁美好的感情。

1804年，有个英国人把这首歌收进了他的书中。于是，《茉莉花》成为了中国第一首通过书流传到国外的民歌。1926年，著名的意大利音乐家普契尼（Giacomo Puccini，1858—1924）的歌剧《图兰朵》（*Turandot*）开始在意大利演出，并获得巨大成功。由于普契尼把《茉莉花》作为这部歌剧的主要音乐之一，所以随着这个歌剧的流传，"茉莉花"的芳香也飘到了世界各地。

其实，《茉莉花》本来有三段歌词，分别唱的是茉莉花、金银花和玫瑰花三种花。1957年，一位音乐家把这首歌从唱三种花改成只唱茉莉花，就成了我们今天听到的这首《茉莉花》。现在中国的重大活动中经常会演唱《茉莉花》这首歌。

赞美 (zànměi) *v.* praise, eulogize

纯洁 (chúnjié) *adj.* pure

流传 (liúchuán) *v.* spread

歌剧 (gējù) *n.* opera

演出 (yǎnchū) *v.* show, perform

芳香 (fāngxiāng) *n.* aroma, fragrance

想一想 Questions

"茉莉花"的芳香是怎么飘到世界各地的？

现在的《茉莉花》和原来的有什么不同？

语言点 Language Points

通过
by means of

1. 这首民歌通过赞美茉莉花，来表现男女之间纯洁美好的感情。

By praising the jasmine flower, this folk song manifests the pure and beautiful emotions between lovers.

"通过"，介词。后面可接名词、动词或小句。表示以人或事物为媒介或手段而达到某种目的。

"通过" is a preposition. It could be used before nouns, verbs or clauses to indicate "achieve a goal through certain means or person".

(1) 他通过一个同事的介绍，认识了小王。

(2) 通过努力学习，他的汉语水平提高得很快。

本来
originally

2. 《茉莉花》本来有三段歌词，分别唱的是茉莉花、金银花和玫瑰花三种花。

Originally, *The Song of Jasmine Flower* consisted of three sets of lyrics, which praised the jasmine flower, the honeysuckle and the rose respectively.

"本来"，副词。是"原先；先前"的意思。可以用在主语或动词前。

"本来" is an adverb meaning "originally", "previously". It can be used before the subject or the verb.

(1) 本来今天我想和朋友去看电影，但是她突然有事不去了。

(2) 他本来计划今年 3 月结婚，但因为工作太忙，改在 10 月了。

练 习 Exercises

1. 判断正误。True or false.

（1）1926年意大利人普契尼的歌剧《茉莉花》开始演出。 （ ）

（2）以前这首歌中有三种花，现在只有茉莉花一种花。 （ ）

（3）现在中国的重大活动中经常会使用《茉莉花》这首歌。（ ）

2. 选择正确答案。Choose the correct answer.

（1）《茉莉花》首先流传到了（ ）。

A. 西班牙　　B. 美国　　C. 英国　　D. 意大利

（2）最早的《茉莉花》里没有（ ）。

A. 茉莉花　　B. 金银花　　C. 兰花　　D. 玫瑰花

小知识 Cultural Tips

茉莉花
Jasmine Flower

茉莉，常绿小灌木，高可达一米。叶色翠绿，花色洁白，香味浓厚，是常见的庭园及盆栽观赏芳香的花卉。茉莉花在许多国家被看作爱情之花或友谊之花。茉莉花清香四溢，能够提取茉莉油，是制造香精的原料。在北方最流行的花茶，就是在绿茶中加入茉莉花制成的。

Jasmine is a genus of evergreen shrubs and can grow as high as one meter. With green leaves, white flowers, and dense fragrance, it is a common ornamental flower for gardens, yards and potted landscapes. Jasmine flower is considered as the flower symbolizing love or friendship in many countries. Its flowers can be used to extract jasmine oil, an ingredient for essence. The most popular flower tea in the north of China is made by mixing green tea and jasmine flowers.

4 倒茶的礼貌

Dào chá de lǐmào

倒茶的礼貌

Etiquette in Serving Tea

你喜欢喝茶吗？
你知道礼貌的倒茶方法吗？

故乡 (gùxiāng) *n.*
hometown

招待 (zhāodài) *v.*
treat, entertain

礼节 (lǐjié) *n.*
ceremony, etiquettes

倒 (dào) *v.*
pour

喝茶对人的身体有很多好处。中国是茶叶的故乡，人们很早以前就有喝茶的习惯。同时，用茶招待客人也是中国人的一个重要礼节。

人们对喝茶的方法非常讲究，倒茶也有一些需要注意的地方。首先，茶杯要非常干净。倒茶之前，要认真地用水洗茶杯，最好用开水烫一下。这样不但卫生，而且对客人也是一种礼貌。

其次，茶叶的多少要合适。茶叶多，茶的味道就会浓一些；茶叶少，茶的味道就会淡一些。所以，最好先问问客人喜欢喝浓茶还是淡茶，然后按照客人的习惯放茶叶。再说水，无论是大茶杯还是小茶杯，水都不能倒太满或太少。

再次，端茶要有礼貌。按照中国的传统习惯，茶杯应该用双手端。其中一只手拿着茶杯，另一只手托住茶杯下面，这样把茶端给客人才是最有礼貌的。

最后，加水也要有礼貌。如果客人茶杯里的茶快喝完了，要及时给客人加水。加水的时候要先给客人加，再给自己加。这样做也表示对客人的尊敬。

烫 (tàng) *v.* rinse with hot water, scald

浓 (nóng) *adj.* strong, thick

淡 (dàn) *adj.* light, thin

端 (duān) *v.* serve, hold sth. level with both hands

托 (tuō) *v.* hold sth. in the open palm

想一想 Questions

语言点 Language Points

讲究
pay attention to, be particular about

1. **人们对喝茶的方法非常讲究，倒茶也有一些需要注意的地方。**

Much attention is paid to the way of drinking tea. There are also some aspects of serving tea which require special attention.

"讲究"，形容词。"要求很高；档次高"的意思。

"讲究" is an adjective that means "be particular about", "high-grade".

(1) 她不讲究吃，也不讲究穿，很随意（suíyì：behave at will）。

(2) 小王一家讲究卫生，房间总是干干净净的。

按照
according to

2. **最好先问客人喜欢喝浓茶还是淡茶，然后按照客人的习惯放茶叶。**

It is advised to ask first the guest whether he likes strong tea or weak tea, and to put tea in the cup according to the preference of the guest.

"按照"，介词。后面可以接名词、动词或小句。表示遵照某种标准。

"按照" is a preposition that can be followed by nouns, verbs or clauses and indicates "in accordance with certain standards".

(1) 按照我们现在的速度，三点以前可以到学校，不会迟到。

(2) 现在，北京的四合院正按照国家的要求进行保护。

练 习 Exercises

判断正误。True or false.

（1）倒茶前最好先洗一下茶杯。 （ ）

（2）给客人倒茶，应该把水倒满。 （ ）

（3）给客人端茶，应该两只手同时拿着茶杯。 （ ）

（4）加水时，应该先给客人加。 （ ）

（5）中国是茶叶的故乡。 （ ）

（6）为了表示尊敬客人，就要多放茶叶。 （ ）

小知识 Cultural Tips

中国的龙井茶

Chinese Longjing Tea

中国是茶叶的故乡，以茶待客是中国人的基本习惯。茶叶主要有绿茶、红茶、黑茶、乌龙茶、黄茶和白茶等品种，龙井茶是著名的绿茶，产于中国南部名城杭州西湖一带，它具有“色绿、香浓、味甘、形美”的特点。常喝龙井茶可以提神止渴、防止高血压。龙井茶历史悠久，最早可以追溯到唐代（公元618—907年），一千多年来，它已经逐步成为中国名茶并享誉世界。

China is the home of tea, where it is a custom to treat guests to a cup of tea. In China, there are several kinds of tea, such as green tea, black tea, fermented tea, Wulong tea, yellow tea and white tea. Longjin tea is a famous green tea produced in the West Lake region of Hangzhou in South China. It has four unique features, namely emerald green color, rich fragrance, sweet and pure taste, and exquisite shape. Frequent drinking of Longjin tea helps to refresh oneself, quench one’s thirst as well as restrain the blood pressure. Longjin tea has a very long history, which dates back to the Tang Dynasty (618 AD—907 AD). For over a thousand years, it has become famous in China and abroad.

5 Tiěchǔ móchéng zhēn 铁杵磨成针

An Iron Pestle Can Be Ground into a Needle

一个人要成功，最需要什么？答案也许有很多。但做好任何事情都需要坚持，需要努力。

诗人 (shīrén) *n.*
poet

逃课 (táokè) *v.*
play truant, skip classes

老婆婆 (lǎopópo) *n.*
old woman, granny

粗 (cū) *adj.*
thick

唐代大诗人李白小时候不喜欢上学，常常逃课，到街上去玩儿。

一天，李白又没有去上学，跑到城外去玩儿。看着城外的美景，李白心想：每天在屋里读书多没意思！出来玩儿多好啊！

他走着走着，看见一个白发的老婆婆，正在磨一根非常粗的铁杵。李白走过去问："老婆婆，您在做什么？"

“我要把这根铁杵磨成一根绣花针。”老婆婆对李白笑了笑，又低下头继续磨。

“绣花针？”李白又问，“是缝衣服用的绣花针吗？”

“当然！”

“可是，铁杵这么粗，什么时候才能磨成细细的绣花针呢？”

老婆婆反问李白：“滴水可以穿石，铁杵为什么不能磨成绣花针呢？”

“可是，您的年纪这么大了……”

“只要我比别人更努力，就没有做不到的事情。”

老婆婆的话让李白很惭愧。回家后，他再没有逃过课，每天学习都特别用功，终于成为一名伟大的诗人。

这个故事告诉我们：无论做什么事情，只有不停地努力，才会成功。

铁杵 (tiěchǔ) *n.*
iron pestle

绣花针 (xiùhuāzhēn) *n.*
embroidery needle

缝 (féng) *v.*
sew, stitch

细 (xì) *adj.*
thin

反问 (fǎnwèn) *v.*
ask in reply

滴水穿石(dīshuǐ chuānshí)
Constant dropping wears away a stone.

穿(chuān) *v.*
penetrate

惭愧(cánkuì) *adj.*
ashamed

用功(yònggōng) *adj.*
diligent

想一想 Questions

语言点 Language Points

到……去……
go … for doing …

1. **唐朝大诗人李白小时候不喜欢上学，常常逃课，到街上去玩儿。**

Li Bai, the famous poet of the Tang Dynasty, didn't like school when he was a child. He often skipped classes and went on the street for fun.

"到……去……"，两个动词连用，后一动词（短语）表示的动作行为是前一动词表示的动作行为的目的。

"到……去……" is used to connect two verbs, with the latter referring to the purpose of the former.

(1) 上个星期六，我到上海去看一个朋友了。

(2) 周末，我们打算到商店去买点儿东西。

为什么
why

2. **老婆婆反问李白："滴水可以穿石，铁杵为什么不能磨成绣花针呢？"**

The granny asked Li Bai in reply, "If constant dropping can wear away a stone, why can't the iron pestle be ground into a needle?"

由"为什么"、"什么"等构成的特指问句带上反问语气，就构成了反问句，不需要对方作出回答。

Wh-questions with words like "为什么" (why) or "什么" (what) become rhetorical questions if said in the tone of rhetorical questions. There is no need to answer it.

(1) 你知道迟到不好，为什么又迟到了呢？（不应该迟到）

(2) 这件事，我什么时候告诉她了？（我从来都没有告诉她）

练习 Exercises

1. 判断正误。True or false.

（1）李白小时候每天都去上学，从来不去街上玩儿。 （ ）

（2）老婆婆要把铁杵磨成做衣服用的针。 （ ）

（3）李白觉得老婆婆要做的事情很简单。 （ ）

2. 选择正确答案。Choose the correct answer.

（1）李白觉得老婆婆不能成功，不是因为（ ）。

A. 铁杵很粗　　B. 绣花针很细

C. 老婆婆不努力　　D. 老婆婆年纪太大了

（2）李白听了老婆婆的话，（ ）。

A. 很生气　　B. 很高兴　　C. 不好意思了　　D. 不明白

小知识 Cultural Tips

唐代的大诗人李白

Li Bai—a Great Poet of the Tang Dynasty

李白，字太白，号青莲居士，是中国唐代最伟大的浪漫主义诗人。李白的诗歌题材多种多样，丰富和发展了盛唐时期英雄主义的时代主题。其诗风雄奇豪放，想象丰富，语言流转自然，音律和谐多变。他的诗歌达到了中国古代诗歌艺术的高峰。

Li Bai, alias Taibai and Green Lotus Hermit, is the greatest poet of Romanticism in the Tang Dynasty.

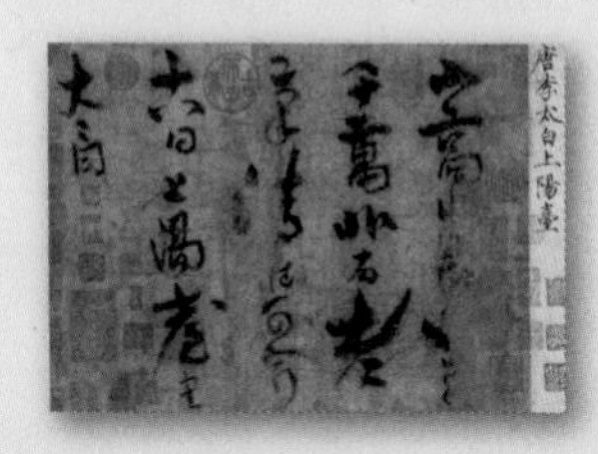

His poems vary in subjects and styles, which have enriched and promoted the theme of heroism in the prosperous Tang Dynasty. The grandness, majesty, free spirit, rich imagination, and the smooth and natural language, and the diverse yet harmonious rhymes manifested in his poems made them the pinnacle of ancient Chinese poetry.

6 Qǐng wèi kuājiǎng dàoqiàn
请为夸奖道歉
Please Apologize for Making Compliments

美丽的外貌不是个人的本领，
通过努力取得成绩才是值得夸奖的。

访问 (fǎngwèn) *v.* visit

教授 (jiàoshòu) *n.* professor

夸奖 (kuājiǎng) *v.* praise

朋友给我讲过这样一个故事。

他到一个国家访问，周末到一位教授家中做客。进屋看到教授五岁的小女儿，满头金发，漂亮的眼睛像海水一样蓝。收下朋友带去的中国礼物后，小女孩儿微笑道谢，朋友禁不住夸奖说："你长得这么漂亮，真是可爱极了！"

教授当时没有说什么，但是女儿走了之后，她变得严肃起来：“你伤害了我的女儿，你要向她道歉。”朋友特别吃惊：“我是真心地夸奖她，怎么会伤害她呢？”教授摇摇头：“你是因为她的漂亮而夸奖她，但她的外貌取决于我和她父亲，和她的努力没有关系。可孩子还很小，不会明白。你的夸奖会让她认为这是她的本领。如果她认为漂亮值得骄傲，就会看不起不太好看的孩子。”教授接着说，“其实，你可以夸奖她的微笑和有礼貌，这是她自己努力的结果。所以，请为你刚才的夸奖道歉。”

“后来呢？”我禁不住问朋友。

“后来，我就向教授的小女儿道了歉，同时表扬了她的微笑和有礼貌。”朋友说，“从那以后，每当我看到漂亮的孩子，我都会对自己说，不要夸奖他们的外貌，因为每一次不合适的夸奖，都可能伤害孩子。”

严肃 (yánsù) *adj.* serious

外貌 (wàimào) *n.* appearance

本领 (běnlǐng) *n.* ability

骄傲 (jiāo'ào) *adj.* proud

看不起 (kànbuqǐ) *v.* look down upon

想一想 Questions

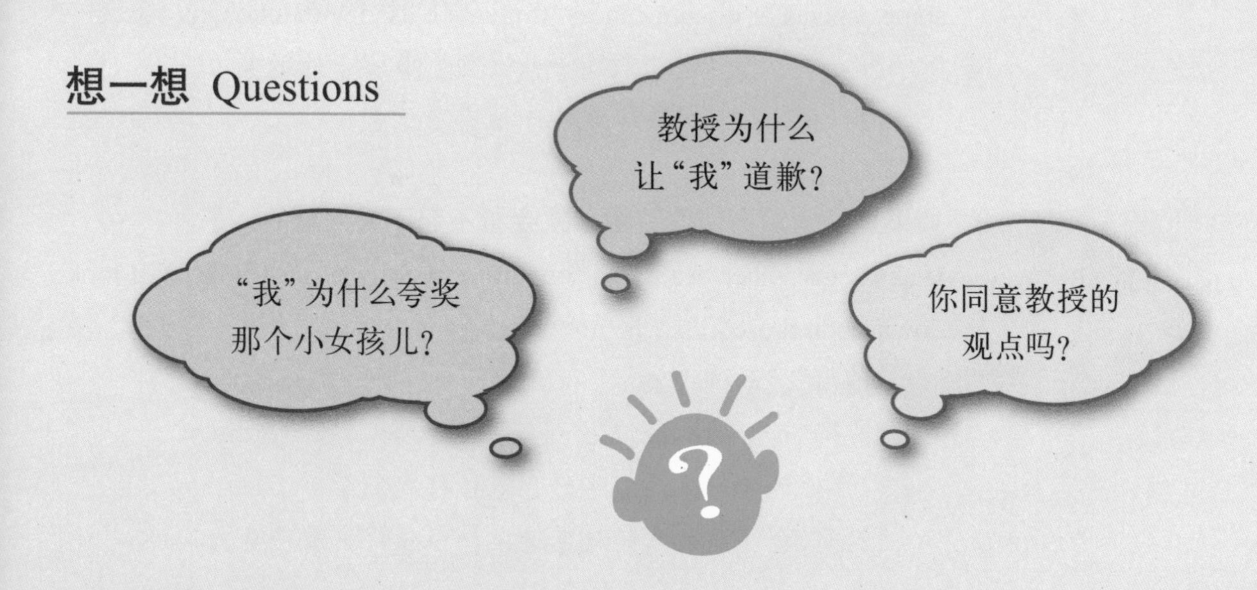

语言点 Language Points

禁不住
can't help doing

1. 朋友禁不住夸奖说："你长得这么漂亮，真是可爱极了！"

My friend can't help praising, "You are so beautiful. You look extremely lovely!"

"禁不住"，动词。是"控制不了；忍不住"的意思。后边可带动词、名词或小句。

"禁不住" is a verb meaning "cannot control", "be bursting to". It can be used before verbs, nouns or clauses.

（1）这个电影太让人感动了，很多人都禁不住流下了眼泪。

（2）听到这个好消息，她高兴得禁不住跳了起来。

取决于
depend on

2. 她的外貌取决于我和她父亲，和她的努力没有关系。

Her appearance depends on me and her father. It has nothing to do with her own effort.

"取决于"，动词。由某方面或某种情况决定，后面必带宾语。

"取决于" is a verb used to show something is determined by some aspects or circumstances. It must be used with an object after it.

（1）一个人的成功取决于什么呢？取决于他的努力。

（2）买什么样的房子取决于他有多少钱。

值得
be worthy of

3. 如果她认为漂亮值得骄傲，就会看不起不太好看的孩子。

If she regards her beauty as something worthy of pride, she will look down upon those kids who are not so good-looking.

"值得"，动词。表示"有价值；有好处"的意思。

"值得" is a verb that means "be valuable", "be worthy of".

（1）他的学习方法非常好，很值得我们学习。

（2）四合院是北京的特色建筑，很值得去看一看。

练 习 Exercises

判断正误。 True or false.

（1）教授认为夸奖孩子的外貌对孩子没有好处。 （ ）

（2）教授认为朋友应该夸奖孩子的礼貌。 （ ）

（3）孩子的外貌和她自己的努力没有关系。 （ ）

（4）从那以后，朋友不再夸奖孩子的外貌了。 （ ）

小知识 Cultural Tips

适当地夸奖
Proper Compliments

中国的父母大多愿意别人夸奖自己的孩子漂亮可爱。即使孩子不漂亮，听了别人并不由衷的夸奖，也会礼貌地表示谢意。以前中国人教育孩子多奉行“棍棒底下出孝子”、“不打不成才”的原则，现在人们观念改变了，提倡赏识教育，加之多为独生子女，家长们又开始夸奖过度。不夸不行，夸多了也不行，夸奖的学问还是不少的。

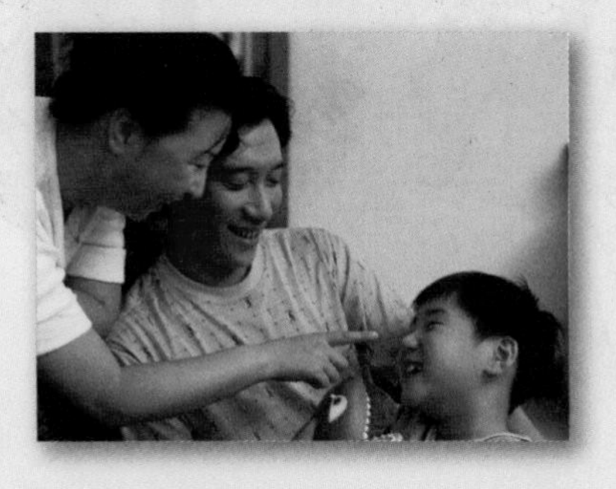

Most Chinese parents will be pleased if their children are complimented as cute and lovely. Even if the compliments are just made out of courtesy and their kids are not good-looking at all, they will express gratitude politely. In the past, Chinese parents educated their children according to the principle that “only spanks and scoldings will nurture a filial and talented kid.” However, nowadays people have a different idea and appreciation education is advocated. In addition, most kids are the only child in the family and parents often praise their kids excessively. Neither too much nor too little praise is good for the children. It’s really a matter worthy of careful consideration.

7 Wángzǐ sàimǎ
王子赛马

The Horse Racing of the Princes

从相反的角度（jiǎodù：angle, point of view）思考问题，有时会有不一样的效果。

继承人 (jìchéngrén) *n.* successor

赛马 (sàimǎ) *v.* race horses

终点 (zhōngdiǎn) *n.* end point

一个国王有两个儿子。为了确定自己的继承人，他决定让两个儿子举行一场赛马比赛。但是这场比赛不是比谁跑得快，而是比谁的马最后到达终点。胜利者就成为继承人。

他给了两个儿子不相上下的两匹马，让他们各挑一匹。比赛开始，两个儿子同时上路了。

在路上，两个王子都很磨蹭，谁也不想快走。后来，两个王子都下马休息，不再走了。再后来，两个王子干脆躺下休息，看样子谁也不会走了。

这样下去也不是办法。小王子突然想出了一个主意，站起来就骑上一匹马，跑了出去。大王子一愣，很快就明白了，于是也急急忙忙起来，也骑上一匹马，去追小王子。

不用说，胜利者是小王子，他成了国王的继承人。

你知道小王子的好办法是什么吗？

答案就是逆向思维！他不是让自己的马跑得更慢，而是让哥哥的马跑得更快。怎么能让哥哥的马跑得更快呢？小王子骑上大王子的马跑起来，大王子的马先到终点，自己的马当然就后到了。

胜利者 (shènglìzhě) *n.* winner

磨蹭 (móceng) *v.* dillydally, act slowly

愣 (lèng) *v.* be surprised

不用说 (bùyòngshuō) *conj.* needless to say

逆向思维 (nìxiàngsīwéi) reverse thinking

想一想 Questions

语言点 Language Points

不相上下
be equally matched

1. **他给了两个儿子不相上下的两匹马，让他们各挑一匹。**

He gave his two sons two equally matched horses to choose one for themselves respectively.

“不相上下”，表示水平程度差不多，分不出高低、好坏等。

“不相上下” is used to show that levels or degrees are roughly the same and hard to differentiate.

（1）这两个乒乓球队员的水平不相上下，比赛结果很难说。

（2）现在我的汉语已经和中国人不相上下了。

干脆
simply

2. **再后来，两个王子干脆躺下休息。**

And at last, the two princes simply lay down to have a rest.

“干脆”，副词。“索性”的意思，表示简单果断地（作出决定）。

“干脆” is an adverb that means “might as well”, and (make up one’s mind) “simply and decidedly”.

（1）如果你不太愿意和他一起旅游，干脆就不要答应。

（2）现在去电影院也来不及了，干脆明天再去吧。

练 习 Exercises

选择正确答案。Choose the correct answer.

（1）两个王子的马，（　　）。

A．小王子的比大王子的马好　　B．大王子的比小王子的马好

C．差不多　　D．都不太好

（2）小王子要骑哥哥的马，是因为（　　）。

A．哥哥的马比自己的好　　B．哥哥的马快

C．他想让哥哥的马先到终点　　D．他想让国王高兴

（3）国王让小王子做继承人，是因为他（　　）。

A．知道大王子的马不好　　B．最喜欢小王子

C．希望聪明的人当国王　　D．不太聪明

小知识 Cultural Tips

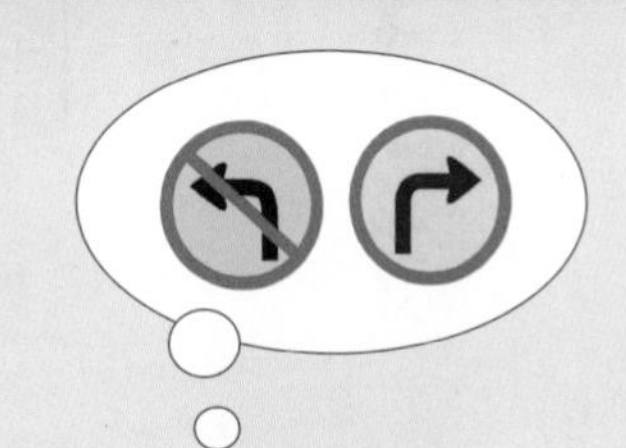

逆向思维
Reverse Thinking

人们习惯于沿着事物发展的方向去思考问题并寻求解决办法。其实，对于某些问题，尤其是一些特殊问题，从结论往回推导，倒过来思考，从求解回到已知条件，反过来想或许会使问题简单化，这就是逆向思维。

Most people are conditioned to think and seek solutions basing on common sense. In fact, for some problems, especially uncommon ones, to deduce backward from the conclusion, i.e., from the solution to the known conditions, will simplify the problem. This is what we call "reverse thinking".

8 Xiānggǎng de dàpáidàng 香港的大排档

Sidewalk Snack Booths in Hong Kong

如果你在晚上出来逛街，可能会看到路边摆出了很多桌子，人们在那里边吃边喝边聊。那就是大排档。

汇集 (huìjí) *v.* come together, converge

露天 (lùtiān) *n.* the open air

香港是一个各种文化汇集的地方，有很多东西都是外来的，但是大排档却不是。

所谓大排档，是指一种餐饮方式。店主在人行道或小巷中摆出几张桌子，客人就在这种露天或半露天的环境下吃饭。大排档里食物的种类很多，大都比较便宜。大排档一般从傍晚开始营业，直到深夜才结束，这是大排档的一大特色。

对于大排档的来历，大概很多经常吃大排档的人都不知道。其实，大排档在第二次世界大战后才出现。当时一些香港公务员在战争中受伤或死去，政府为了帮助他们和他们的家人，就发给他们一种执照，允许他们在路边开小饭馆。由于食物好吃又便宜，所以这些小饭馆非常受欢迎。在广东话里，“档”是“小摊”的意思，又因为政府发的执照很大，所以大家就把这些在路边的小饭馆叫做“大牌档”。20 世纪 60 年代是大排档的黄金时期，来吃饭的人很多，所以人们把“大牌档”改成了“大排档”，并一直用到现在。

到了 20 世纪 80 年代，政府认为大排档影响香港的交通和卫生，所以把大排档请进了饭店。但是它仍然能够吸引不少人，因为它改变的只是环境而不是味道。

营业 (yíngyè) *v.* do business

来历 (láilì) *n.* origin

公务员 (gōngwùyuán) *n.* civil servant

受伤 (shòushāng) *v.* get injured

执照 (zhízhào) *n.* license

允许 (yǔnxǔ) *v.* permit

小摊 (xiǎotān) *n.* stall, booth

世纪 (shìjì) *n.* century

年代 (niándài) *n.* a decade

仍然 (réngrán) *adv.* still, as before

想一想 Questions

语言点 Language Points

却
but

1. 但是大排档却不是。

But the sidewalk snack booth is not (from foreign countries).

"却"，副词。表示转折，语气比较轻，常用在主语后。

"却" is an adverb that indicates a gentle transition. It is usually used after subjects.

（1）这家公司的人虽然不多，却个个都很能干。

（2）她家住得最远，却总是每天第一个到学校。

所谓
so-called

2. 所谓大排档，是指一种餐饮方式。

The so-called sidewalk snack booth is a way of buying food and drink.

"所谓"，形容词。是"通常所说"的意思，常用于提出需要解释的词语，然后再加以解释。

"所谓" is an adjective that means "what is known as", and is often used to bring forward the word to be explained afterward.

（1）所谓"中国通"，就是对中国的各种情况非常熟悉的外国人。

（2）我认为，所谓"幸福"，就是一个人对自己的生活感到满足。

练习 Exercises

1. 判断正误。True or false.

（1）大排档最早出现在香港。 （ ）

（2）大排档的食品一般都很贵。 （ ）

（3）晚上营业是大排档的一个特色。 （ ）

2. 选择正确答案。Choose the correct answer.

（1）大排档发展的黄金时期是（　　）。

A. 二战之后　B. 20 世纪 60 年代　C. 20 世纪 80 年代　D. 现在

（2）下面的说法正确的是（　　）。

A. 大排档一般在室内营业

B. 大排档常常在白天营业

C. 大排档是香港的“特产”（tèchǎn：special local product）

D. 大排档进入饭店以后，味道改变了

小知识 Cultural Tips

香港得名于香江，位于中国华南沿海，由香港岛、九龙半岛、新界内陆地区及 260 多个大小岛屿组成。1997 年 7 月 1 日，香港正式回归中华人民共和国，成为中国的一个特别行政区，按照“一国两制”的方针，仍然享有高度的自治权。由于优越的地理位置和国际资本的不断注入，香港已发展成为世界金融贸易中心之一。同时，香港还是亚洲最受欢迎的旅游胜地之一。

Named after the Xiangjiang River, Hong Kong is located in the coastal area of the southeastern part of China and consists of Hong Kong Island, Kowloon Peninsula, New Territories and over 260 islands of different sizes. On July 1, 1997, Hong Kong was officially returned to the administration of the People's Republic of China and became a Special Administrative Region, which enjoys a high degree of autonomy under the guideline of "One Country, Two Systems". Due to its favourable geographic location and constant investment from all over the world, Hong Kong has become one of the world's financial and commercial centers. Meanwhile, Hong Kong is also one of the most popular tourist spots in Asia.

9 Yì měiyuán de qìchē 一美元的汽车

The One Dollar Car

“一美元买一辆豪华汽车。”

如果在报纸上看到这样的广告，你会相信吗？

登 (dēng) *v.* publish

豪华 (háohuá) *adj.* luxurious

少妇 (shàofù) *n.* young married woman

发票 (fāpiào) *n.* receipt

美国的一家报纸上登了这样一个广告：“一美元买一辆豪华汽车。”

哈利看到广告，心想：今天不是四月一号啊！但他还是带着一美元去了。

在一栋非常漂亮的房子前面，哈利敲开了门。

一位少妇为他打开门，问清楚后，少妇带哈利来到车库，指着一辆豪华汽车说："就是它。"

哈利脑子里闪过的第一个念头就是："是坏车。"就问："太太，我可以试试吗？"

"当然可以！"于是哈利开着车转了一圈，一切正常。

"这辆轿车不是偷来的吧？"哈利要求看一下发票，少妇拿给他看了。

一切都没问题后，哈利付了一美元。当他开车要离开的时候，心里仍然非常好奇。他问："太太，您能告诉我这是为什么吗？"

少妇叹了一口气："唉，实话跟你说吧。我丈夫死了。他把一切都留给了我，只有这辆车，是属于他那个情妇的。但是，他把这辆车的拍卖权交给了我，拍卖的钱交给他的情妇。所以，我决定卖掉它，一美元就可以。"

哈利恍然大悟，他开着车高高兴兴地回家了。路上，哈利碰到了他的朋友汤姆。汤姆好奇地问起这辆车的来历。等哈利说完，汤姆一下子坐在了地上："啊！一周前我就看到这个广告了！"

好奇 (hàoqí) *adj.* curious

叹气 (tànqì) *v.* sigh

情妇 (qíngfù) *n.* mistress

拍卖 (pāimài) *v.* auction

恍然大悟 (huǎngrán-dàwù) suddenly realize

想一想 Questions

哈利看到广告时，相信这是真的吗？

哈利的朋友听了哈利的话后是什么心情？

语言点 Language Points

闪过（一个）念头
an idea flashing through one's mind

1. 哈利脑子里闪过的第一个念头就是："是坏车。"

The first idea that flashed through Harry's mind was, "The car is broken."

"闪过（一个）念头"，是"（一个）想法突然出现在脑子里"的意思。

"闪过（一个）念头" means "an idea flashing through one's mind".

（1）看到朋友在国外的照片，我的脑子里突然闪过一个念头：明年我要出国！

（2）她学习汉语一年了，最近她脑子里常常闪过"去中国留学"的念头。

属于
belong to

2. 只有这辆车，是属于他那个情妇的。

Only this car belongs to his mistress.

"属于"，动词。是"归某一方所有"的意思。

"属于" is a verb that means something belongs to somebody.

（1）哈利，现在这辆车属于你了。

（2）最后的胜利属于小王子。

练习 Exercises

1. 判断正误。True or false.

（1）"一美元买一辆汽车"是一个愚人节的玩笑。　（　）

（2）那辆汽车有一点毛病，所以很便宜。　（　）

（3）汽车的拍卖权不是这位少妇的。　（　）

（4）哈利的朋友不相信这个广告是真的。　（　）

2. **选择正确答案。**Choose the correct answer.

（1）那辆豪华汽车少妇只卖一美元，是因为（　　）。

A. 车有些毛病　　B. 这辆车太旧了

C. 她不想给那个情妇很多钱　　D. 她的丈夫让她卖一美元

（2）这一美元最后应该给（　　）。

A．这位少妇　　B. 少妇的丈夫

C. 少妇丈夫的情妇　　D. 哈利

（3）哈利的朋友坐在地上，是因为（　　）。

A. 他突然身体不舒服　　B. 他当初不相信这个广告，现在非常后悔

C. 他没有看报纸，错过了机会　　D. 他忘了这件事，很遗憾

小知识 Cultural Tips

生活中充满奇迹
Life is Full of Miracles

一般人看到一美元汽车的广告，可能都会习惯性地认为是个骗局。文中的哈利如果不去实地看一下，豪华轿车怎么能到手呢？生活中充满奇迹，什么事都可能发生。有人买几块钱的彩票中了上千万元的大奖；有人因收到一条错误的短信收获一段美丽的爱情……

It would normally be considered a trap when one sees an advertisement about a car for only one dollar. If Harry, as mentioned in the text, did not go and check it by himself, how would he get a limousine? Life is full of miracles, and anything is possible. With a lottery ticket that costs only several *yuan*, someone wins a ten-million prize; someone is blessed with sweet love because of a text message sent to the wrong person …

10 Dà dǎoyǎn, xiǎo gùshi
大导演，小故事

Great Director, Petty Stories

很多成功人士常常因为工作忙而没有时间照顾家人，
但大导演李安却不是这样。

事业 (shìyè) *n.*
career

精彩 (jīngcǎi) *adj.*
brilliant, wonderful

艰苦 (jiānkǔ) *adj.*
arduous, difficult

靠 (kào) *v.*
rely on, depend on

在事业上，李安是国际著名的大导演，拍过很多精彩的电影，也得过很多大奖。在生活中，他是一位关心妻子儿女的好丈夫、好父亲。

成功前，李安生活得很艰苦。他没有工作，全靠妻子在外面工作养家。当他的电影《喜宴》在柏林电影节上获得金熊奖后，

朋友请他吃饭，为他庆祝。谁知道菜刚一上桌，李安竟然大哭起来。朋友觉得很奇怪，问他怎么回事。原来，李安想起了在纽约家里的妻子和孩子，想起了全家人一起度过的苦日子。李安很希望在这个时候能跟他们一起庆祝。

即使是很有名以后，李安仍然抽空照顾妻子儿女。有一天，李安夫妇去市场买菜。路上有人认出了李安，忍不住对他妻子说："你命真好，先生现在还有空儿陪你买菜！"没想到妻子却说："不是他陪我，是我今天特意抽空陪他！"原来李安成为大导演后还一直坚持买菜做饭，不愿意让妻子太辛苦，难怪他们夫妻俩的感情这么好。

庆祝 (qìngzhù) *v.*
celebrate

竟然 (jìngrán) *adv.*
unexpectedly

度过 (dùguò) *v.*
spend, get through

抽空 (chōukòng) *v.*
find the time to do sth.

命 (mìng) *n.*
life, fate

陪 (péi) *v.*
accompany

特意 (tèyì) *adv.*
specially,
for a special purpose

想一想 Questions

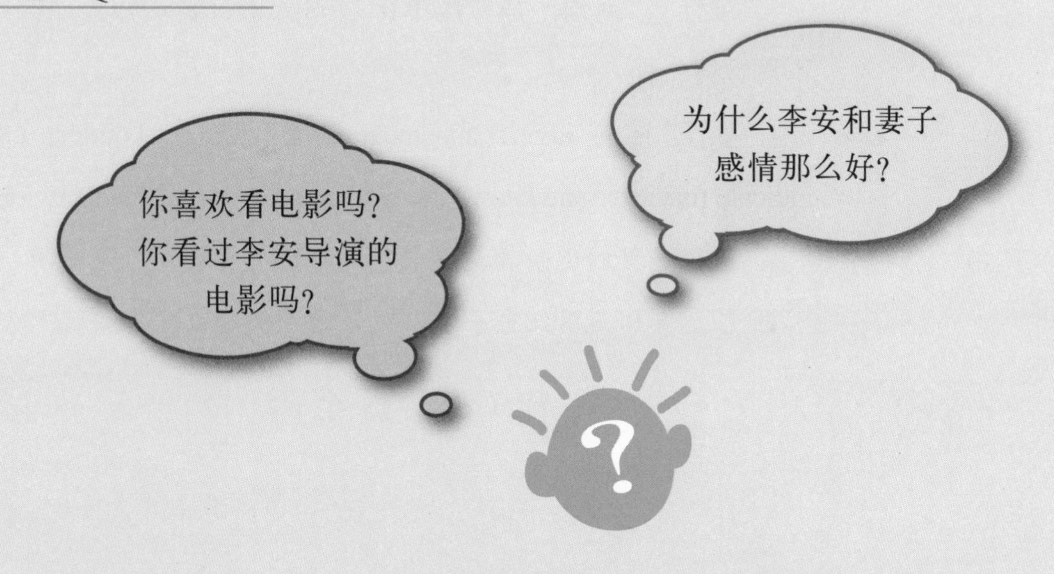

语言点 Language Points

原来
it turns out that/to be

1. 原来李安成为大导演后还一直坚持买菜做饭，不愿意让妻子太辛苦。

It turns out that, even after he becomes a great director, Ang Lee continues to do grocery shopping and cook because he does not want his wife to work too hard.

"原来"，副词。表示忽然明白了，发现从前不知道的情况。

"原来" is an adverb that means someone suddenly realizes the situation or circumstances unknown before.

(1) 难怪他这么高兴，原来他下周要去中国旅行。

(2) 杰克今天没来上课，原来他生病了。

难怪
no wonder

2. 难怪他们夫妻俩的感情这么好。

No wonder they are so devoted to each other.

"难怪"，副词。是"怪不得"的意思，表示知道原因以后，不再觉得奇怪。

"难怪" is an adverb that means "怪不得"(no wonder), used to indicate that after one knows the reason, he is not puzzled any longer.

(1) 这里的风景真是美极了，难怪有那么多人来旅游。

(2) 女朋友跟他分手了，难怪他今天这么不高兴。

练 习 Exercises

1. 判断正误。 True or false.

（1）李安是一位著名的电影导演。 （　　）

（2）成功以前，李安生活得很好。 （　　）

（3）因为《喜宴》获奖了，所以李安和朋友一起吃饭。 （　　）

2. 选择正确答案。 Choose the correct answer.

（1）和朋友一起吃饭时，李安哭了，是因为（　　）。

A. 他很饿　B. 他非常激动　C. 他想起他的妻子和孩子　D. 饭太贵了

（2）有了名之后，李安仍然坚持去买菜，是因为他（　　）。

A. 时间很多　B. 喜欢买菜　C. 不想让妻子太累　D. 不想让妻子孤独

小知识 Cultural Tips

李安
Ang Lee

李安（Ang Lee），著名电影导演，1954 年出生在中国台湾。1993 年推出的《喜宴》在柏林电影节上荣获金熊奖，并获得了奥斯卡奖最佳外语片提名。2000 年的作品《卧虎藏龙》创下了美国有史以来外语片的最高票房纪录。2006 年凭借《断背山》成为首位夺得奥斯卡最佳导演奖的华人导演。

Ang Lee, a famous movie director, was born in Taiwan of China in 1954. *Wedding Banquet* directed by him in 1993 won the Golden Bear Award at Berlin International Film Festival, as well as a nomination for the Best Foreign Language Film at the Academy Awards. *Crouching Tiger*, *Hidden Dragon*, filmed in 2000, set the box office record of foreign films in America. In 2006, he won the Academy Award for Best Directing with *Brokeback Mountain* and became the first Chinese director to win the award.

11 Zhōngguó "gǒu" hé Xīfāng "gǒu"
中国"狗"和西方"狗"

Chinese and Western 'Dogs'

狗是生活中常见的动物。
但是不同的文化对它的态度却很不一样。

紧密 (jǐnmì) *adj.* close, intimate

差异 (chāyì) *n.* difference

宠物 (chǒngwù) *n.* pet

狗是和人们生活联系很紧密的动物，但是中西方文化对狗的看法却有很大的差异。

虽然现在很多家庭都很喜欢狗，把狗当作宠物，但是在过去，中国人一般认为狗是看家的动物，不是人们的宠物。因此与狗有关的词语大多是贬义的，如"走狗"、"狗眼看人低"等。

而在西方文化中，人们对狗有特别的感情，认为狗十分可爱、聪明和忠实。狗被视为人类最好的朋友，在主人家中的地位很高，有专门的狗屋、狗粮、各种狗玩具，有的人甚至把狗当成家庭成员。英语中还常常用“dog”（狗）指人，意思相当于“fellow”（朋友）。例如，“a lucky dog”（幸运儿），就带有喜爱的意思。英语中还有其他许多与狗有关的习语，也大多是褒义的，如“love me，love my dog”（爱屋及乌）。

另外，一些与狗有关的汉语和英语习语，虽然看起来一样，但文化含义却完全不同。比如“老狗”和“old dog”，“老狗”是骂人的话，“old dog”却是指“年纪大、经验丰富的人”。

贬义 (biǎnyì) *n.* derogatory meaning

忠实 (zhōngshí) *adj.* faithful

专门 (zhuānmén) *adv.* specially

成员 (chéngyuán) *n.* member

习语 (xíyǔ) *n.* idiom

褒义 (bāoyì) *n.* complimentary sense

含义 (hányì) *n.* meaning

想一想 Questions

语言点 Language Points

大多
most

1. 因此与狗有关的词语大多是贬义的。

Consequently, most words and expressions associated with dogs are of derogatory meanings.

"大多"，副词。"大部分；大多数"的意思。

"大多" is an adverb that means "mostly", "the majority of".

(1) 参加比赛的大多是今年新来的学生。

(2) 在大排档卖的食物大多很便宜。

相当于
equivalent to

2. 英语中还常常用"**dog**"（狗）指人，意思相当于"**fellow**"（朋友）。

In English, the word "dog" is often used to refer to people with the meaning equivalent to that of "fellow".

"相当于"，表示对比的双方（数量、价值、条件等）差不多。

"相当于" indicates "an almost equal or equivalent status" (in quantity, value, qualification, etc.) between two parties compared.

(1) 熊猫的 20 岁相当于人的 70 岁。

(2) 这件衣服的价钱相当于我一个月的工资。

练 习 Exercises

判断正误。True or false.

（1）过去中国人常用狗来看家。 （ ）

（2）汉语里有很多和狗有关的词都带有贬义。 （ ）

（3）狗在西方国家很受欢迎。 （ ）

（4）英语中用狗指人时，表示不喜欢这个人。 （ ）

（5）汉语和英语中有关狗的词，看起来一样，意思也一样。 （ ）

小知识 Cultural Tips

动物比喻

Animals in Figures of Speech

各种语言中都常常用动物来比喻人，汉语中也有很多动物常被用来比喻不同特点的人。中国人常说一个聪明的人像“猴子”一样机灵；而一个懒惰的人常被骂为“懒猪”。如果一个人身体很棒，会有人夸他比“牛”还要壮，而瘦人常被称为“瘦猴”。人们觉得那些恶毒的人像“毒蛇”一样，而凶狠的人像“狼”一样。

Animals are frequently used in figures of speech of different languages to describe people. In Chinese, many animals are also used to liken to people of different traits. Chinese often describe someone smart as a “monkey”. A lazy person is usually compared to a lazy “pig”. If someone is strong, he will be praised as stronger than an “ox”. Thin people are often called a thin “monkey”. Those malicious people are compared to “vipers” and fiendish people are like “wolves”.

12 Nánrén xiàchú hǎochù duō 男人下厨好处多

Cooking Is Good for Men

你会做饭吗？在你家，
是父亲做饭还是母亲做饭？

负责 (fùzé) *v.* be responsible for

充分 (chōngfèn) *adj.* enough, sufficient

中国家庭的传统是"男主外，女主内"。意思就是，男人负责在外面工作，挣钱养家；女人负责在家洗衣做饭，照顾孩子。而在现代社会中，越来越多的女人也开始工作，她们已经没有足够的时间和精力一个人做家务。因此，不少男人开始帮妻子做一些家务。尤其是在中国南方，很多男人经常下厨，而且能烧一手好菜。他们认为那样可以充分享受家的感觉，不仅可以减轻妻子的负担，还能增进夫妻感情。

另外，男人下厨还对身体健康有好处。最近的研究发现，做饭也是很好的运动。一般来说，人们工作时只运用左脑，但是做饭却可以运用右脑，让人的反应更快，从而起到锻炼身体的作用。另外，做饭可以培养人的判断力。什么时候放油，什么时候放菜，这些都是很有讲究的。做饭还可以培养分析能力。面对一道不熟悉的菜，优秀的厨师一般看一看、尝几口就知道大概应该怎么做。做饭同时也是一门艺术。要做出既好看又好吃的美食，自然也少不了一定的创造力。

享受 (xiǎngshòu) *v.* enjoy

减轻 (jiǎnqīng) *v.* ease

负担 (fùdān) *n.* burden

增进 (zēngjìn) *v.* enhance

反应 (fǎnyìng) *n.* reaction

培养 (péiyǎng) *v.* foster, cultivate

分析 (fēnxī) *v.* analyse

创造力 (chuàngzàolì) *n.* creativity

想一想 Questions

语言点 Language Points

起到……作用
have the function of …

1. 做饭却可以……起到锻炼身体的作用。

But cooking ... has the function of exercising one's body.

"起到……作用",是"有……作用","达到……目的"的意思。

"起到……作用" means "have the function of …", "achieve the goal of …"

(1) 多跟中国人聊天可以起到提高汉语水平的作用。

(2) 音乐有时候可以起到让人放松的作用。

从而
thus

2. 做饭却可以运用右脑,让人反应更快,从而起到锻炼身体的作用。

But cooking can exercise the right hemisphere of the brain ... thus it has the function of exercising one's body.

"从而",连词。"从而"前面的小句表示原因、方法等,后面的小句表示结果、目的等。

"从而" is a conjunction. The clause before it gives "reasons", "ways of doing things", while the clause after it gives "results", "purposes", etc.

(1) 他打算骑自行车旅行,从而更好地了解中国。

(2) 运动可以让人出汗,从而起到减肥的作用。

练 习 Exercises

1. 判断正误。True or false.

（1）“男人工作挣钱，女人做家务”是中国以前的传统。 （ ）

（2）做饭可以锻炼人的大脑。 （ ）

（3）在中国，南方男人经常做饭，北方男人根本不做饭。 （ ）

（4）做饭很简单，不需要创造力。 （ ）

2. 讨论题。Discussion.

你觉得“男主外，女主内”这样的家庭分工怎么样？

小知识 Cultural Tips

妇女在中国的地位

Women's Social Status in China

在 1949 年以前，由于中国的儒家传统文化认为“女子无才便是德”，普通人家妇女很少接受教育，大多在家辅佐丈夫、教育孩子，经济上没有独立地位，不得不依附于男性，社会地位低下。到了近代，由于西方民主思想的传入，妇女的地位逐步提高，可以和男性一样学习和工作。今天，中国男女完全平等，在教育、就业、参政议政等方面享有同等的权利。在大多数家庭里，妇女婚后还要继续工作，所以夫妻都要做一些家务。

Before 1949, women from common families received little education due to the Confucian tradition that “ignorance is a woman's virtue”. Most of them stayed at home to take care of their husband and educate their children. Lack of independent economic status led to women's dependence on men and their low social status. In modern times, however, with the introduction of western democracy, women's status was gradually elevated and they could study and work just as men did. Today, Chinese men and women enjoy equal social status in that they receive equal rights to education, job opportunities and participation in political affairs. In most families, the husband and the wife share the housework because the wife usually continues to work after getting married.

13

Nián huà

年画

New Year Pictures

春节的时候，你会在很多中国人的家门上看到一幅画：一个胖娃娃抱着鲤鱼（lǐyú：carp）。那就是中国过年时贴的传统年画。

逐渐 (zhújiàn) *adv.* gradually

风俗 (fēngsú) *n.* custom

农历 (nónglì) *n.* lunar calendar

年画是中国画的一种。在不同的地方，年画的名称也很不相同，现在逐渐地简称为“年画”。根据传统风俗，中国人在农历的腊月二十五这一天要在窗上和墙上贴上各种年画，希望新一年的生活能更加美好。

年画有很长的历史，它最早是古代的门神画。传说从前有一位皇帝生病时，梦里常听到奇怪的声音，所以睡不好觉。后来，他的两位将军每天晚上站在门口守卫，夜里果然平安无事了。皇帝认为两位将军太辛苦了，所以就让人把这两位将军的样子画在门上，称为“门神”。

后来，年画的内容也变得多种多样，各种美好的事物或者民间传说都可以作为主题。每到过春节的时候，差不多每家都会买几张年画。从大门到室内，贴满了各种象征吉祥富贵的年画，其中最流行的要算是抱着鲤鱼的胖娃娃了。年画对春节的热闹气氛也起了不少的作用呢。

腊月 (làyuè) *n.* the twelfth month of the lunar year

皇帝 (huángdì) *n.* emperor

将军 (jiāngjūn) *n.* general

守卫 (shǒuwèi) *v.* guard

民间 (mínjiān) *n.* folk

传说 (chuánshuō) *n.* legend

象征 (xiàngzhēng) *v.* symbolize, signify

吉祥 (jíxiáng) *adj.* lucky, auspicious

气氛 (qìfēn) *n.* atmosphere

想一想 Questions

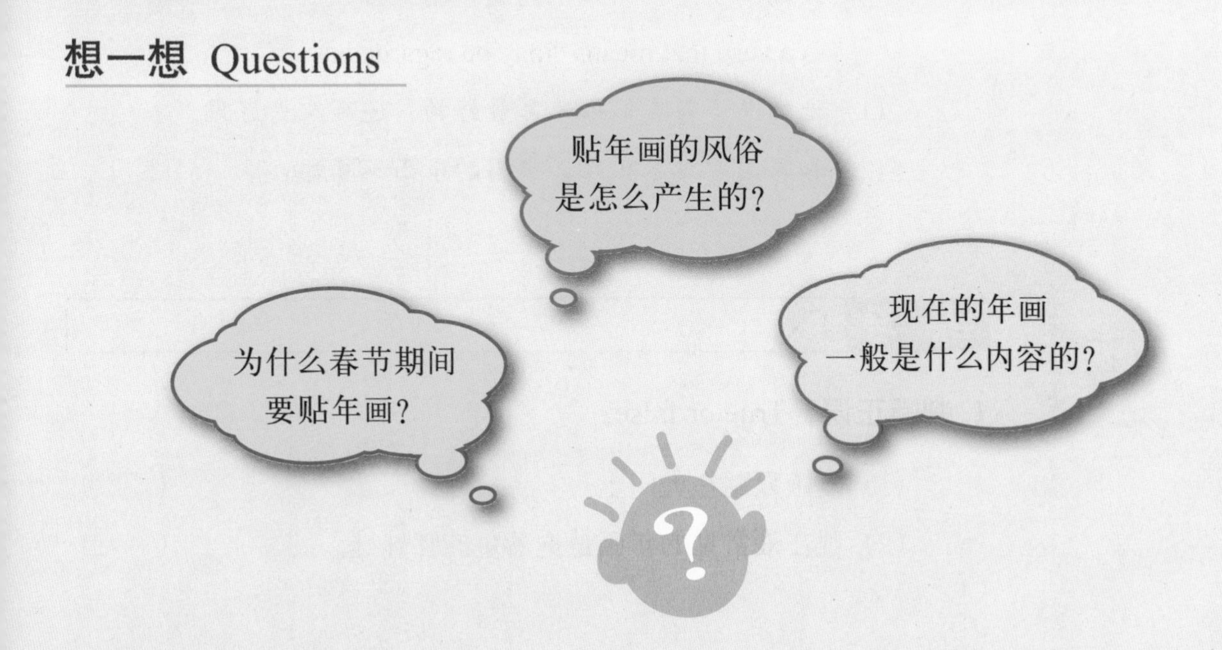

语言点 Language Points

果然
surely enough

1. 他的两位将军每天晚上站在门口守卫，夜里果然平安无事了。

His two generals guarded his gate every night and surely enough it became tranquil and peaceful.

"果然"，副词。表示事实和之前想象的或者判断的一样。

"果然" is an adverb used to indicate the reality is exactly the same as the presumption or prejudgement.

（1）听说这部电影很不错，看了以后觉得果然很好。

（2）大家都相信他一定能赢，最后他果然得了第一名。

算
be regarded as

2. 最流行的要算是抱着鲤鱼的胖娃娃了。

The picture of a chubby child holding a carp is regarded as the most popular one.

"算"，动词。是"可以认为是"的意思。

"算" is a verb that means "may be regarded as ...".

（1）他的汉语在我们班不算最好的，还有人更好呢。

（2）和美国、日本相比，中国的东西不算贵。

练 习 Exercises

1. 判断正误。True or false.

（1）年画只贴在大门上。 （ ）

（2）现在最常见的年画是抱着鱼的胖娃娃。 （ ）

2. 选择正确答案。Choose the correct answer.

（1）按照传统，贴年画应该在（　　）。

A. 春节前一天　B. 春节当天　C. 春节前五天　D. 春节前一个月

（2）门神画画的是（　　）。

A. 两位将军　B. 抱着鲤鱼的胖娃娃　C. 一位皇帝　D. 一位老人

（3）现在，中国人贴年画是（　　）。

A. 为了夜里睡觉能更安全　B. 希望新一年的生活更好

C. 因为喜欢画儿　D. 为了让房子看起来更漂亮

小知识 Cultural Tips

杨柳青年画

Yangliuqing New Year Pictures

说到年画，不能不提天津的杨柳青。杨柳青是一个镇名，这个镇的民间木版年画产生于元末明初。到了清代中期，当时某个画店一年生产的成品就达2000件，每件500张，共达百万幅。杨柳青全镇连同附近的30多个村子，画店一家接着一家，家家都制作年画，各地来订画、买画的客商非常多，使杨柳青成了名副其实的绘画之乡。

Speaking of New Year pictures, one has to mention Yangliuqing, a town in Tianjin. This town specializes in woodcut folk New Year pictures, starting from late Yuan or early Ming dynasty. By the middle of the Qing Dynasty, one painting store there could turn out 2 000 woodcut products a year, with 500 copies of pictures from each, which added up to millions of copies. In Yangliuqing and over 30 villages around it, many painting stores make New Year pictures, attracting merchants from all over the country. This makes Yangliuqing a famous producer of paintings.

14 Gěi māma de yì fēng xìn 给妈妈的一封信

A Letter to Mum

你经常给爸爸妈妈写信吗？
你有心里话会跟爸爸妈妈说吗？

一心一意 (yīxīn-yīyì)
wholeheartedly

任务 (rènwù) *n.*
task

心烦 (xīnfán) *adj.*
vexed

责怪 (zéguài) *v.*
blame

组织 (zǔzhī) *v.*
organize

亲爱的妈妈：

您好！

当您看到这封信时，一定觉得很奇怪，为什么生活在您身边的女儿还要给您写信呢？我想，写信更便于和您讲我的心里话。

妈妈，您为了让我一心一意地学习，什么都不让我做。您总是说："你的任务只有一个——学习。"您知道我听了这些话多心烦吗？

记得有一个星期天，您从市场买回来很多菜。我放下书本，高高兴兴地到厨房打算帮您做一些家务。可是，您却说："放下吧！去复习功课，下次考好一些就行了。"我知道，您是责怪我期中考试没有考好。我扔下菜，跑回自己的房间，伤心地哭了。妈妈，您还记得吗？有一次学校组织我们打扫操场，这对我来说并不难。可是，您为了"疼爱"我，让我在家学习，请假替我去劳动。您知道我的同学们怎么说我吗？您这样每天只让我"读书、读书"，对我的成长有什么好处呢？

妈妈，我知道您非常爱我，但我真的不需要过度的"关照"，因为总有一天，我要一个人面对生活中的困难。请您理解我！

您的女儿：月月

六月三日夜

疼爱 (téng'ài) *v.* love dearly

替 (tì) *v.* take the place of

成长 (chéngzhǎng) *v.* grow up

过度 (guòdù) *adj.* excessive

关照 (guānzhào) *v.* care

理解 (lǐjiě) *v.* understand

想一想 Questions

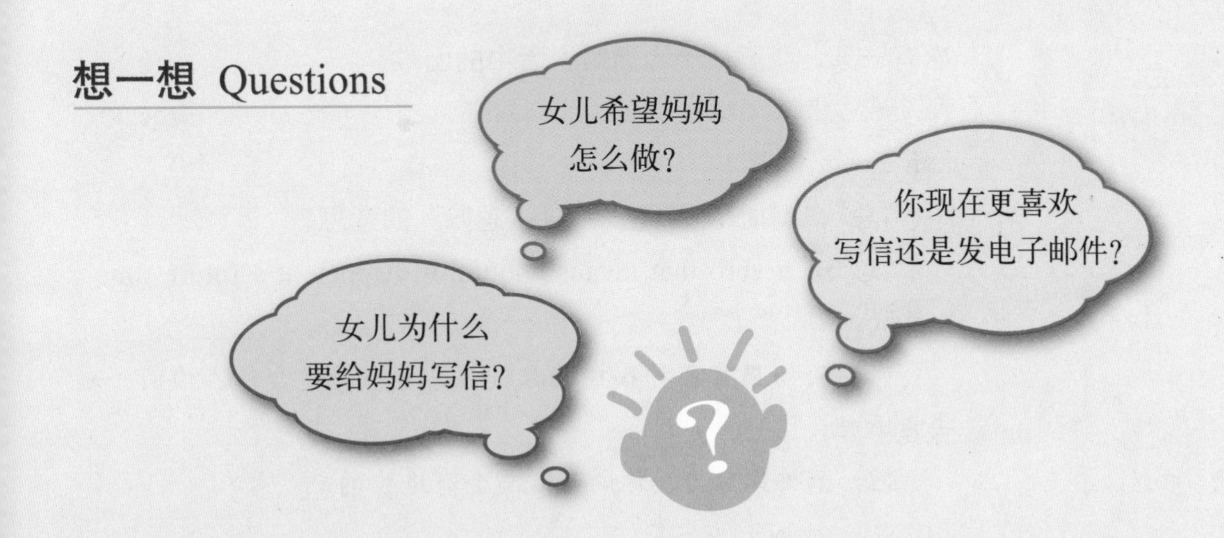

语言点 Language Points

便于
convenient for

1. 写信更便于和您讲我的心里话。

It is much more convenient for me to share my deep thoughts with you in a letter.

“便于”，动词。是“比较容易（做某事）”的意思。

“便于” is a verb with the meaning “convenient for doing something”.

（1）笔记本电脑越来越小，非常便于携带（xiédài：carry）。

（2）咱们互相留下电子邮件吧，这样便于以后联系。

记得
remember

2. 记得有一个星期天，您从市场买回来很多菜。

I remember there was one Sunday when you bought a lot of vegetables from the market.

“记得”，动词。是“想得起来；没有忘掉”的意思。

“记得” is a verb that means “remember”, “have not forgotten”.

（1）记得以前这里非常安静，现在却这么热闹。

（2）记得一年前刚到中国时，我只会说一句“你好”。

总
anyhow

3. 总有一天，我要一个人面对生活中的困难。

Anyhow, there will be one day when I need to face all the difficulties in life by myself.

“总”，副词。“最终一定会；总归”的意思。

“总” is a verb that means “bound to happen at a future time”, “anyhow”.

（1）商场里有各种各样的衣服，总有一件适合你，咱们一起去看看吧。

（2）只要你努力，你的汉语总会有进步的。

练 习 Exercises

判断正误。True or false.

(1)“我”不好意思和妈妈面对面说这个问题，所以写信。　　( )

(2)“我”期中考试没有考好，妈妈没有生气。　　( )

(3) 妈妈不让“我”参加学校的活动，是为了让“我”有更多的时间学习。　　( )

(4)“我”觉得妈妈这样关心我，对“我”没有好处。　　( )

小知识 Cultural Tips

中国的“小皇帝”

‘Little Emperors’ in China

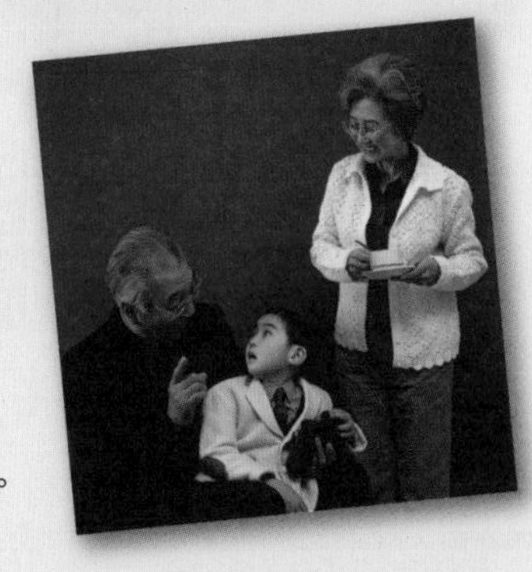

现在的中国家庭绝大多数都只有一个孩子，因此形成了父母以及祖父母、外祖父母围绕着一个孩子打转的情况。大人们对孩子的照顾无微不至，甚至代替孩子做很多应该由他们自己做的事情。这样的溺爱，会对孩子的身心成长造成不好的影响，会惯出很多任性、骄傲、自私、没有独立生活能力的“小皇帝”。不过现在很多家庭都已经意识到了这一点。

There is only one child in most Chinese families nowadays, and the parents and grandparents of both sides focus all their attention on this only child. The adults often take meticulous care of the children, even doing many things which should be done by children themselves. Such doting love will harm the physical and mental development of the children, bringing up “little emperors”, who are capricious, arrogant, selfish and dependent on others. Fortunately, many families have realized this problem now.

15

Shuōshuo Sānlǐtún

说说三里屯

About Sanlitun

如果你到过北京，我想你一定听说过三里屯吧？
那么三里屯是个什么样的地方呢？

休闲 (xiūxián) *v.* have leisure

娱乐 (yúlè) *v.* entertain

位于 (wèiyú) *v.* be located

说到北京的三里屯，无论是留学生还是在北京工作的外国人，都没有人不知道。这个因酒吧而闻名的地方，现在已经成为外国人休闲娱乐的重要场所了。

三里屯位于朝阳区东部，因离城区三里而得名。1962 年这个地方开始建大使馆，20 世纪 60 ~ 70 年代建成外交公寓群。

三里屯逐渐发展成为外交人员居住、购物和进行外事活动的重要社区。现在的三里屯附近有包括加拿大、澳大利亚、法国、比利时、德国等在内的 79 个国家的使馆。

1995 年，两个从日本留学回来的年轻人在这里建起了第一家酒吧。经过十多年的发展，目前三里屯周围三千米的地区已经有几十家不同风格、不同特色的酒吧。在这里你可以尽情地选择自己喜爱的风格——浪漫的、热情的……

三里屯是酒吧街，但又不仅仅是酒吧街，还是音乐街。到了晚上，酒吧里有很多乐队为人们激情地歌唱。很多著名的歌手也常常来三里屯演出。此外，三里屯还是一条美食街、服装街。现在的三里屯是各种人、各种文化、各种生活态度汇集的地方。人们在这里寻找着、享受着属于自己的那份满足感。

大使馆 (dàshǐguǎn) *n.* embassy

公寓 (gōngyù) *n.* apartment

外事 (wàishì) *n.* foreign affairs

社区 (shèqū) *n.* community

尽情 (jìnqíng) *adv.* to one's heart's content

浪漫 (làngmàn) *adj.* romantic

激情 (jīqíng) *n.* passion, enthusiasm

想一想 Questions

语言点 Language Points

是……还是……
whether ... or ...

1. 无论是留学生还是在北京工作的外国人，都没有人不知道。

There is no one who does not know Sanlitun, be they foreign students or foreigners working in Beijing.

"是……还是……"，表示选择。

"是……还是……" means "whether ... or ...".

(1) 对这件事，你是赞成还是反对？

(2) 是去酒吧还是去电影院，我们还没有决定。

因……而……
because of

2. 这个因酒吧而闻名的地方，现在已经成为外国人休闲娱乐的重要场所了。

This area, famous because of its bars, has become an important place of recreation and entertainment for foreigners.

"因……而……"组成一个动词短语，表示原因。

The construction of "因……而……" can be used as a verb phrase to indicate "reason".

(1) 大熊猫因样子可爱、数量少而成为中国的国宝。

(2) 他爸爸经常因一点儿小事而生气，所以孩子们都很怕他。

练 习 Exercises

1. 判断正误。 True or false.

（1）因为这个地方离城区三里，所以叫“三里屯”。 （ ）

（2）很多外国人在三里屯附近工作和生活。 （ ）

（3）三里屯酒吧街里常常有音乐表演。 （ ）

（4）现在的三里屯，不只有酒吧，还是美食、服装汇集的地方。 （ ）

2. 选择正确答案。 Choose the correct answer.

（1）三里屯是从（ ）开始有酒吧的。

A. 1962 年　　B. 20 世纪 60 年代　　C. 20 世纪 70 年代　　D. 1995 年

（2）下面不是三里屯特点的是（ ）。

A. 音乐街　　B. 书店街　　C. 服装街　　D. 美食街

小知识 Cultural Tips

中国人的夜生活
Chinese People's Night Life

改革开放 30 年来，中国城市的夜景越来越美，中国人晚间的活动也越来越丰富多彩。人们不只是呆在家里看电视、打扑克。现在，年轻人可以去酒吧和朋友聚会，也可以去健身房锻炼身体。情侣们可以去 KTV 尽情歌唱，也可以去电影院看夜场电影。老年人也不甘寂寞，舞场里、街心花园里、活动室里都有老人们跳舞、唱歌、运动的身影。

Over the past thirty years since the implementation of the policy of reform and opening-up, night views of Chinese cities have become more beautiful and Chinese people's nightlife has also become more colorful. At night, people no longer just stay at home, watching TV and playing poker. Young people can go to the bars and get together with friends, or go to the gyms to do exercises. Lovers can go to KTV or watch movies. The old also hate to be left alone. They dance, sing or exercise in dancing halls, small parks by the streets and community activity rooms.

16 Shí'èr shēngxiào wèishénme méiyǒu māo? 十二生肖为什么没有猫?

Why Does the Cat Eat the Mouse?

中国的十二生肖有十二种动物，都有哪些动物呢？

牛 (niú) *n.* ox

虎 (hǔ) *n.* tiger

兔 (tù) *n.* rabbit

中国的十二生肖是：鼠、牛、虎、兔、龙、蛇、马、羊、猴、鸡、狗、猪。你知道为什么有老鼠却没有猫吗？这里有个故事。

很早以前，人们要选十二种动物作为人的生肖，每年一种动物。可是动物太多了，怎么办呢？大家商量后选了个日子，让动物们在这一天来报名，最先报名的十二种动物就是十二生肖。

猫和老鼠是邻居，又是好朋友。它们都想去报名。猫说："咱们得早点儿起床去报名，可是我爱睡觉，怎么办呢？"老鼠说："没关系，没关系。我一醒就去叫你，咱们一块儿去。"猫听了很高兴，说："你真是我的好朋友，谢谢你了。"

到了报名的那天早晨，老鼠很早就醒了。可是它光想着自己的事，忘了好朋友猫，就自己去报名了。结果，老鼠被选上了。而猫因为起床太晚了，所以没有被选上。猫因此很生气。从此以后，猫见了老鼠就要吃它。

其实这只是个故事，并不是真的。十二生肖里有老鼠却没有猫，是因为猫是从国外传到中国的。中国出现"十二生肖"这个词的时候，还没有"猫"这个词呢。

龙 (lóng) *n.* dragon

蛇 (shé) *n.* snake

羊 (yáng) *n.* goat

猴 (hóu) *n.* monkey

鸡 (jī) *n.* rooster

猪 (zhū) *n.* pig

报名 (bàomíng) *v.* sign up for

传 (chuán) *v.* spread

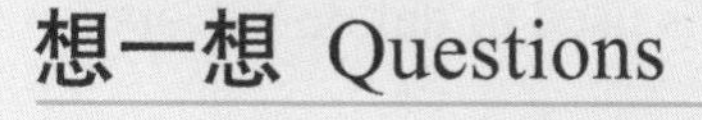

想一想 Questions

根据故事，
十二生肖里为什么有老鼠却没有猫？实际上又是为什么？

十二生肖有哪些动物？你知道自己的生肖是什么吗？

语言点 Language Points

得（děi）
need to

1. 咱们得早点儿起床去报名。

We need to get up early to sign up.

“得（děi）”，助动词。表示事实上或情理上的需要，相当于“应该；必须”的意思。用于口语。

“得（děi）” is an auxiliary verb that indicates “a factual or reasonable need”, similar to “应该” and “必须”. It is used in oral Chinese.

（1）教授，你伤害了我的女儿，你得向她道歉。

（2）谢谢你的建议，但是我得自己考虑考虑。

光
only

2. 可是它（老鼠）光想着自己的事，忘了好朋友猫，就自己去报名了。

The rat only had itself in mind and forgot its good friend cat. It went to sign up by itself.

“光”，副词。是“只”的意思，用来限定范围。

“光” is an adverb that means “only”. It is used to define a scope.

（1）这件事很难，光靠你一个人不行。

（2）学习汉语不光要多看多写，还要多听多说。

练习 Exercises

判断正误。True or false.

(1) 鼠、鸡、鱼都是生肖中的动物。 ( )

(2) 因为猫容易忘事，所以它让老鼠第二天去叫它。 ( )

(3) 老鼠没有去叫猫，是因为它不想让猫成为生肖。 ( )

(4) “猫”这个词是在十二生肖产生以后出现的。 ( )

小知识 Cultural Tips

本命年
Birth Year

生肖本来是用于纪年的一套符号，后来发展成了生肖信仰。其中非常重要的一部分是中国人“本命年”的观念。本命年是按照十二生肖循环推算出来的。每过 12 年，人们就要遇到自己的本命年，所以本命年是 12 岁、24 岁、36 岁等。中国人认为本命年是凶年，需要趋吉避凶。所以每到本命年，不论大人小孩都要买红腰带系上，称为“扎红”。中国人还很重视老人的 60 岁生日，称为“花甲”。花甲是一生中第六个本命年，也是干支纪年的一个轮回，必须好好庆祝，以此寄托人们企求健康长寿的美好愿望。

Originally, Shengxiao was a set of symbols used to designate years. Later, it developed into a belief. The most important part of it is the concept of “birth year”. One’s birth year is calculated circulatively according to the twelve animals. Therefore, every Chinese will have his or her birth year every twelve years, namely when they are of the age 12, 24, 36, etc. However, the Chinese consider their birth year as a bad year during which certain ill matters should be shunned. Thus, people who are in their birth year, be they children or adults, will wear red belts during this year. This is called “Red Bind”. Chinese also attach great importance to the sixtieth birthday, which is called “Huajia”. It is the sixth birth year in one’s life, and also the first transmigration of the system of designating years by the Heavenly Stems and Earthly Branches. It is worthy of a grand celebration by which people express their longing for health and longevity.

17 Nánwàng de Yúrénjié
难忘的愚人节
An Unforgettable April Fool's Day

你喜欢和朋友开玩笑吗？
有时候，和别人开玩笑可能最后却捉弄了自己。

捉弄 (zhuōnòng) *v.* fool

郑重 (zhèngzhòng) *adj.* serious, solemn

宣布 (xuānbù) *v.* announce

不知从什么时候开始，中国的大学校园里也开始流行起一个外国人的节日——“愚人节”了。每年的四月一日，校园里到处都在“说谎”，每个人都享受着捉弄别人的快乐。

下面是最让我难忘的一个愚人节。

那时，我是我们班的班长。那天早上，我一进教室，就郑重地宣布："今天下午我们有英语考试，大家要好好准备！""真的吗？""老师没有告诉过我们呀？"同学们问。"这你们还不懂吗？老师是想知道你们平时学习是不是很努力，就想做一次临时测验。她当然不会告诉你们了。"教室里立刻安静下来，紧接着，传来一阵阵朗读英语的声音。同学们有的在背课文，有的在记语法，有的在写生词。看到他们又紧张又认真的样子，我真想笑。

下午上英语课了，英语老师微笑着走进教室。让我没想到的是，老师竟然真的对我们说："同学们，今天我们做一次临时测验，老师想了解一下你们平时的学习情况。请大家准备一下，三分钟以后，我们开始考试。"

同学们都向我投来感谢的目光，然后就开始准备考试了。我呢，好像突然被人泼了一盆冷水，傻了。

临时 (línshí) *adj.* temporary

测验 (cèyàn) *n.* test

紧接着 (jǐnjiēzhe) *adv.* immediately

朗读 (lǎngdú) *v.* read aloud

投 (tóu) *v.* cast

目光 (mùguāng) *n.* look, sight

泼 (pō) *v.* splash

想一想 Questions

语言点 Language Points

安静下来
become quiet

1. 教室里立刻安静下来。

The classroom becomes quiet at once.

"形容词 + 下来"，表示一种状态开始并继续。

The construction of "adj.+下来" indicates "the beginning of a state which will proceed".

(1) 晚上六点多了，天渐渐黑下来了。

(2) 他跑得太累了，速度已经慢下来了。

泼冷水
pour cold water on somebody

2. 我呢，好像突然被人泼了一盆冷水，傻了。

As for me, I felt as if someone poured cold water on me and I was left dumfounded.

"泼冷水"，指打击人的热情、破坏人的情绪。

"泼冷水" means "discourage", "make somone feel bad".

(1) 你应该多鼓励孩子，而不是总给他泼冷水。

(2) 没有一个朋友支持他参加中文歌曲比赛，这给他泼了一盆冷水。

练 习 Exercises

判断正误。 True or false.

（1）这个故事发生在四月二日。　　（　　）

（2）“我”知道今天有英语测验。　　（　　）

（3）同学们不相信“我”的话，都没有准备测验。　　（　　）

（4）今天真的没有英语测验。　　（　　）

（5）同学们很感谢“我”的帮助。　　（　　）

小知识 Cultural Tips

中国人过“洋节”

Foreign Festivals in China

随着中国外语学习者的增多，外国文化对中国的影响也在逐渐加大。越来越多的外国节日开始在中国流行起来。人们可以利用这些外国节日放松娱乐一下。同时，商家也都利用节日的机会进行促销。如今，圣诞节、情人节、母亲节、愚人节等外国节日在中国人，特别是年轻人当中很有影响。

As the number of foreign language learners increases, the influence of foreign cultures becomes stronger and stronger in China. More and more foreign festivals have become popular among the Chinese today. People can relax and entertain themselves on the occasions of all these foreign festivals. Meanwhile, businessmen also take these festivals as opportunities to promote sales. Nowadays, foreign festivals, such as Christmas Day, Saint Valentine's Day, Mother's Day and April Fool's Day, are quite popular among Chinese people, especially among the young.

18 Diànnǎo gōngsī de qīngjiégōng
电脑公司的清洁工

A Cleaner at a Computer Company

每个人都能成功。重要的是，你能不能找到一条属于自己的成功之路。

特长 (tècháng) *n.* special skill

厕所 (cèsuǒ) *n.* toilet, washroom

面试 (miànshì) *v.* interview

比西想去一家很大的电脑公司找一份工作。可是他没有什么特长，只能做打扫厕所的清洁工。

面试以后，公司的人告诉他，在一起“考试”的十个人里，他打扫的厕所最干净，公司对他很满意。如果明天收到公司发给他的电子邮件，他就可以来上班了。

这时候，他不好意思地说："我没有电脑，也没有电子邮箱。"公司的人很吃惊，只好告诉他，在这家公司，没有电子邮箱的人等于不存在，所以公司不能让他来工作。比西非常失望。那时他身上只有十美元。他去商店买了十千克的土豆，然后到每家门口，问他们要不要买土豆。

没想到，两个小时后他的土豆就卖光了，人们对这种送到家门口的土豆非常欢迎。他的手里一下子就有了二十美元。他开始认真地做这种生意，不停地努力加上一点儿运气，使他的生意越做越大，不但买了车，还请了二十多个工人。五年后，他建立了一个很大的公司。有了这个公司，人们在自己的家门口就可以买到新鲜的蔬菜。

一天，他去买保险。当保险公司的人问他的电子邮箱时，他再次说："我没有电脑，也没有电子邮箱。"保险公司的人说："您有这样一个大公司，却没有电子邮箱。您想想，如果您有电子邮箱，用它可以做多少事！"

他微笑着回答："对，可以做电脑公司的清洁工。"

电子邮件 (diànzǐ yóujiàn) *n.* email

等于 (děngyú) *v.* be equal to

存在 (cúnzài) *v.* exist

失望 (shīwàng) *adj.* disappointed

生意 (shēngyi) *n.* business

运气 (yùnqi) *n.* luck

建立 (jiànlì) *v.* establish, set up

保险 (bǎoxiǎn) *n.* insurance

想一想 Questions

比西去那家电脑公司工作了吗？为什么？

比西最后是怎么成功的？

语言点 Language Points

什么
whatever

1. 他没有什么特长，只能做打扫厕所的清洁工。

He has no special skills and can only work as a cleaner for washrooms.

"什么"，代词。指示不确定的事物或人。

"什么" is a pronoun that refers to a person or thing without being specific.

(1) 你听，外面好像有什么声音。

(2) 今天我有点儿不舒服，所以没吃什么东西。

光
(sell) out, (use) up

2. 没想到，两个小时后他的土豆就卖光了。

Unexpectedly, he sold out all his potatoes two hours later.

"光"，形容词。表示"没有了；一点儿不剩"。

"光" is an adjective that means there is nothing left.

(1) 昨天买的水果已经都吃光了，今天我再去买点儿。

(2) 他很快就花光了父亲留给他的钱。

练习 Exercises

1. 判断正误。True or false.

(1) 比西没去电脑公司工作，因为他打扫的厕所不干净。(　　)

(2) 比西去电脑公司找工作以前卖过土豆。(　　)

(3) 比西卖蔬菜挣了钱，当了老板（lǎobǎn：boss）。(　　)

(4) 现在比西有电子邮箱了。(　　)

(5) 比西觉得如果他有电子邮箱，就没有今天的成功。(　　)

2. **选择正确答案。** Choose the correct answer.

(1) 根据短文，下面说法正确的是（　　）。

A. 电脑公司的清洁工可以不会用电脑

B. 离开电脑公司后，比西去卖保险了

C. 人们不需要送到家门口的土豆

D. 比西因为没有电子邮箱而不能在电脑公司工作

(2) 下面不是比西成功原因的是（　　）。

A. 能把新鲜蔬菜送到人们的家门口　B. 认真地从小生意开始做

C. 经常买保险　D. 自己不停地努力，加上一点儿运气

小知识 Cultural Tips

晋商
The Merchants of Jin (Shanxi)

晋，中国山西省的简称，是中国商业文化的发源地。晋商是中国历史上著名的商人群体，他们以讲究诚信、善于管理著称。在14—19世纪，他们的经营领域和活动范围达到了鼎盛，各种商号、银行遍布全国，甚至到达欧洲、日本、东南亚以及阿拉伯国家。他们在中国的商业界称雄长达500年之久，使地处内陆的山西一时间成为“海内最富”。他们倡导的“诚信为本、以义制利”的经商理念也成为中国商业文化的核心内容。

Jin, short for Shanxi, is the cradle for Chinese commercial culture. *Jinshang* (Shanxi merchants) was a famous merchant group in Chinese history, best known for their honesty and good management. From the 14th to the 19th century, their scope of business reached a climax with different kinds of firms and banks all over the country, even as far as Europe, Japan, Southeast Asia and Arabian countries. They ruled the business world in China for as long as 500 years and made the inland Shanxi province “the richest part of the country”. Their principle that “honesty is the basic policy and profit should be made with integrity” has become the core value of the Chinese commercial culture.

19 这山望着那山高

Zhè shān wàngzhe nà shān gāo

The Grass Is Always Greener on the Other Side of the Fence

中国有句俗语，叫“这山望着那山高”，意思是爬上这座山，觉得另一座山更高。这句话是说人们总是对自己所处的环境不满意，认为别的地方会更好。

婚姻 (hūnyīn) *n.* marriage

牌子 (páizi) *n.* board, sign

帅 (shuài) *adj.* handsome

犹豫 (yóuyù) *v.* hesitate

一家女性婚姻介绍所开业了，女人们可以进去选择一个她喜欢的男人。介绍所门口有一个牌子，上面写着：

每个顾客只能进去一次！介绍所一共六层，越往上，男人的质量越高。不过请注意，顾客只能在任何一层选一个丈夫或者继续上楼，但是不能回到以前到过的楼层。

一个女人来这儿想找一个丈夫。

一层的门上这样写着：第一层，这里的男人有工作。女人连看都不看就上了第二层楼。

二层的门上写着：第二层，这里的男人有工作而且喜欢小孩儿。女人停了一下，又上了第三层楼。

三层写着：第三层，这里的男人有工作，喜欢小孩儿，并且很帅。“啊！”她犹豫了一下，但还是往上走了。

四层写着：第四层，这里的男人有工作，喜欢小孩儿，不但非常帅，还会帮助太太做家务。“天啊！”女人叫道，“我快站不住了！”然后，她还是爬上了第五层楼。

她读着五层的说明书：第五层，这里的男人有工作，喜欢小孩儿，也非常帅，还会做家务，并且非常浪漫。女人非常想留在这一层，但还是充满期待地走向最高一层。

六层出现了一个很大的电子牌，上面写着：你是这层楼的第 456021 位客人。这里没有任何男人，这层楼只是为了证明女人是多么难以满足。

不久，一家男性婚姻介绍所在街对面开业了，经营方式与前一个几乎一样。

第一层的女人长得漂亮。

第二层的女人长得漂亮而且有钱……

结果，第三层到第六层从来没有男人上去过。

说明书 (shuōmíngshū) *n.* introduction, specification

期待 (qīdài) *v.* look forward to, expect

经营 (jīngyíng) *v.* run, operate

想一想 Questions

女性婚姻介绍所对顾客的要求是什么？

那个女人找到满意的丈夫了吗？为什么？

男性婚姻介绍所的情况怎么样？

语言点 Language Points

越……越……
the more …
the more …

1. 介绍所一共六层，越往上，男人的质量越高。

There are altogether six storeys. The higher the storey is, the better the quality of the men is.

"越 A 越 B"，表示在程度上 B 随 A 的变化而变化。

The construction of "越 A 越 B" shows B changes in degree according to the change of A.

(1) 祝你的生意越做越好！

(2) 人越快乐，就越长寿。

难以
difficult to

2. 这层楼只是为了证明女人是多么难以满足。

This storey just testifies how difficult it is to satisfy women.

"难以"，副词。表示不容易做到。多用在动词的前面。

"难以" is an adverb that indicates something is difficult to realize. It is mostly used before verbs.

(1) 听到这个消息，每个人的心情都难以平静。

(2) 他可以去法国留学，但是他没有去，真是让人难以理解。

练　习 Exercises

选择正确答案。Choose the correct answer.

（1）关于女性婚姻介绍所，下面说法正确的是（　　）。

A. 你只可以进去逛一次　　B. 高层的男人质量不如低层的男人

C. 上到高层以后还可以再回到低层　　D. 最高层有条件最好的男人

（2）从那个女人到这家婚姻介绍所的情况，我们可以知道（　　）。

A. 她对第五层的男人没有一点儿兴趣　　B. 已经有很多的女人来过第六层

C. 第六层的男人都被别人选光了　　D. 很多女人在这里找到了丈夫

（3）这个故事想说明（　　）。

A. 女人总是要得太多　　B. 对男人的期待应该高一些

C. 世界上没有完美的人　　D. 男人不喜欢有钱的女人

小知识 Cultural Tips

西施
Xishi

中国的俗语
Chinese Common Sayings

俗语，也叫俗话，是在人们的口语中流传的语句。它既简练又形象。与成语不同，俗语的结构更加灵活多变，内容也更加通俗易懂。俗语最常用的修辞手法有比喻、比拟、借代、夸张等等。比如说，“捡了芝麻丢了西瓜”，用“芝麻”比喻小事，用“西瓜”比喻大事、重要的事；“情人眼里出西施”，用中国古代美女“西施”代指美女。

Common sayings, also called popular sayings, are set expressions circulating orally among people. They are concise and vivid. Different from set phrases or idioms, common sayings are much more flexible in structure and are easier to understand. The figures of speech frequently used in common sayings are metaphor or simile, analogy, metonymy, hyperbole or exaggeration, etc. For example, in “捡了芝麻丢了西瓜 (Pick up the sesame seeds, but take no notice of the watermelons), “芝麻” (sesame) refers to petty things while “西瓜” refers to important things. In “情人眼里出西施” (Beauty lies in the lover’s eyes.)”, “西施” (a beauty in ancient China) refers to beauties in general.

20 Sòng dōngxi 送东西

Give out Relief

郑板桥是中国清朝的著名人物。他既是一位画家，又是一位关心人民生活的好官。

官员 (guānyuán) *n.* official

对联 (duìlián) *n.* couplet

上联 (shànglián) *n.* the first line of a couplet

有一年春节，郑板桥陪一个官员出门办事。路上，有一家人的门上贴着这样一副对联：

上联：二三四五

下联：六七八九

横批：南北

郑板桥看到这副对联后，马上往回走。过了一会儿，他拿着几件衣服、一些肉和菜，还有一些粮食回来了。他推开这家的大门，看见一家人都挤在一张床上，穿着很少的衣服，而厨房里什么吃的东西都没有。郑板桥对他们说："春节到了，我带了这些东西给你们。你们用吧！"那家人看到这些东西，非常感动，也非常高兴，连忙向郑板桥道谢。

等到郑板桥和官员出了这家的门，官员问他："你怎么知道这家人没有衣服，也没有吃的东西呢？"

郑板桥指着这家门上的对联说："上联'二三四五'，里面没有'一'（和'衣'读音相同）。下联'六七八九'，里面没有'十'（和'食'读音相同）。应该是'东西南北'四个方向，横批却只写了'南北'，就是没有'东西'。这个对联不就是告诉我们，他们家缺衣少食，没有东西过春节吗？"

下联 (xiàlián) *n.*
the second line of a couplet

横批 (héngpī) *n.*
a horizontal scroll bearing an inscription to match a couplet

粮食 (liángshi) *n.*
grain, cereals

挤 (jǐ) *v.*
jam, squeeze

感动 (gǎndòng) *v.*
move, touch

想一想 Questions

语言点 Language Points

等到
when, till

1. 等到郑板桥和官员出了这家的门，官员问他……

When Zheng Banqiao and the official got out, the official asked …

"等到"，动词。用在另一个动词或主谓短语的前面，表示主要动作发生的时间。后面常常和"再"、"才"、"就"等配合。

"等到" is a verb used before another verb or subject-predicate phrases to show the time when the main action occurs. It is often followed by "再", "才" and "就".

(1) 我们只好等到老板作出决定再开始工作。

(2) 等到最后一位顾客离开，服装店才关门。

缺
lack, be short of

2. 这个对联不就是告诉我们，他们家缺衣少食，没有东西过春节吗？

Don't the couplets tell us that they don't have enough food and clothing and have nothing for the Spring Festival?

"缺"，动词。表示缺少、不足。可以带名词宾语，也可以单独作谓语，前面加"很"。

"缺" is a verb that indicates "want", "insufficiency". It may take nouns as its objects and can also be used alone as predicate with "很" before it.

(1) 春节快到了，家里还缺对联和"福"字呢。

(2) 这个公司不缺经理，但是清洁工很缺。

练 习 Exercises

判断正误。True or false.

(1) 郑板桥陪着那个官员回家过春节。 ( )

(2) 郑板桥认识那家人。 ( )

(3) 那个官员没有明白那副对联的真正意思。 ( )

(4) 郑板桥很聪明而且很爱帮助别人。 ( )

小知识 Cultural Tips

对联
The Couplets

对联，是汉语的一种独特的艺术形式。对联由上联和下联两个句子组成，分别贴在门的两边，一般用来表达某种愿望或祝福。上下联字数必须相等，内容上也要求对应。上联与下联词语的声调必须按照规定相配合，上下联句子中相同位置的词语词性必须一致。另外，每副对联通常还有一个四个字的横批贴在门的上方与之搭配。

Couplets are a unique art form of the Chinese language. It consists of two lines, which are pasted separately on the sides of a door frame to express certain wishes or blessings. The numbers of characters on each of the two lines are the same and a correspondence in meaning is required. The tones of the characters in each of the lines must be matched according to certain rules. What's more, the part of speech of each character in the second line must be the same as the character on the corresponding place in the first line. In addition, there is a four-character horizontal scroll pasted above the door to sum up the main idea of the two lines.

21 Yǒnggǎn de shuō "bù"
勇敢地说"不"

Dare to Say 'No'

能够对别人说"不"，其实需要很大的勇气（yǒngqì：courage）。

姑妈 (gūmā) *n.*
aunt

随便 (suíbiàn) *adj.*
casual, informal

偏偏 (piānpiān) *adv.*
as luck would have it

马南最近刚刚参加工作，他的姑妈来这个城市看他。马南陪着姑妈在这个小城市里转了转，就到了吃饭的时间。

姑妈一直对他很好，马南想请她好好吃一顿，可他身上只有 20 块钱，只够在一个小饭馆里随便吃一点儿。但是，姑妈却偏偏走进了一家很讲究的餐厅。马南没办法，只好跟着她走了进去。

两人坐下来后，姑妈开始点菜。当她问马南想吃什么时，马南只是吞吞吐吐地说：“随便，随便。”这时，他的心中七上八下，放在口袋里的手紧紧抓着那20块钱。这些钱显然是不够的，怎么办？

可是姑妈一点儿也没注意到马南的不安，她不停地说着这儿的饭菜多么好吃，马南却什么味道都没吃出来。

结账的时间终于到了，服务员拿着账单向马南走来。马南张开嘴，却什么也说不出来。

姑妈笑了。她拿过账单，把钱给了服务员，然后对马南说：“孩子，我知道你的感觉。我一直在等你说‘不’，可你为什么不说呢？要知道，有些时候一定要勇敢地把这个字说出来，才是最好的选择。我这次来，就是想让你明白这个道理。”

吞吞吐吐 (tūntūn-tǔtǔ)
mutter and mumble

七上八下
(qīshàng-bāxià)
be agitated

不安 (bù'ān) *adj.*
restless, worried

账单 (zhàngdān) *n.*
bill

道理 (dàolǐ) *n.*
principle, truth

想一想 Questions

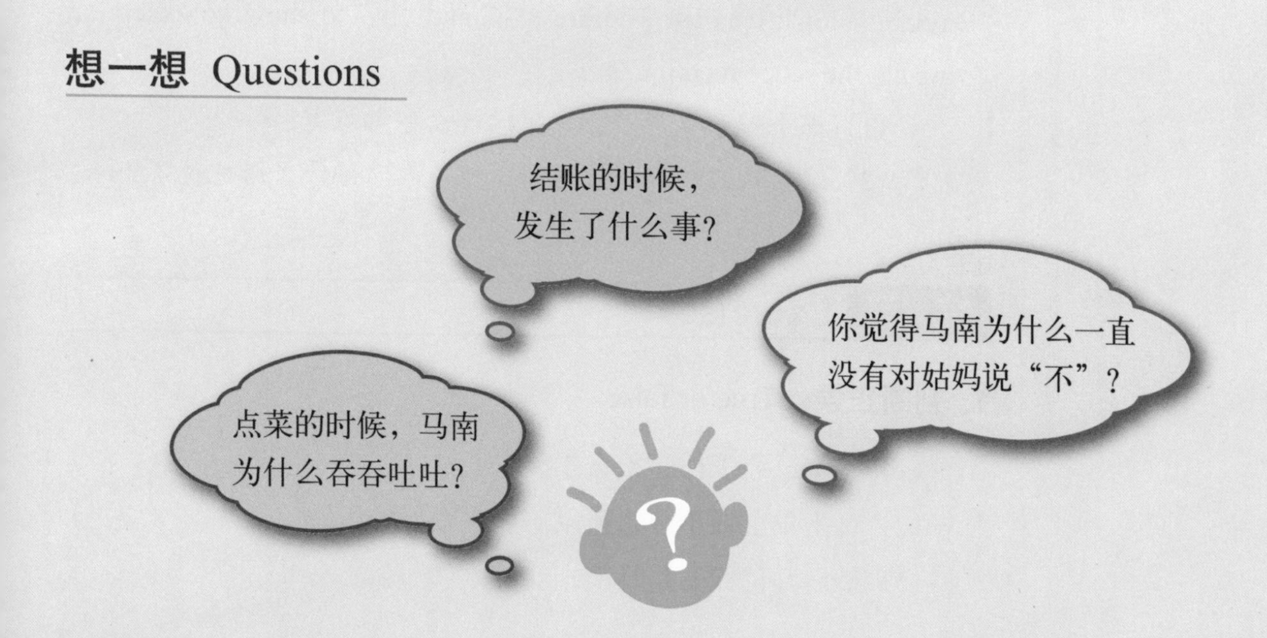

语言点 Language Points

显然
obviously

1. 这些钱显然是不够的，怎么办？

Obviously, the money is not enough. How to cope with this situation?

"显然"，形容词。指情况或道理很容易看出和理解。

"显然" is an adjective. It indicates that the situation or truth is easy to perceive and understand.

(1) 很显然，这是一个善意的谎话。

(2) 这么简单的道理显然不需要我多讲。

什么……都/也……
whatever …

2. 她不停地说着这儿的饭菜多么好吃，马南却什么味道都没吃出来。

She kept saying how delicious the dishes were, but Ma Nan could not enjoy them at all.

"什么"，代词。表示任指。它用在"都"、"也"的前面，表示在所说的范围里没有例外。

"什么" is a pronoun that indicates "unspecified referential relationship". It is used before "都" and "也" to show no exception within the scope mentioned.

(1) 那个孩子觉得"万"字比什么字都难写。

(2) 这家人想向郑板桥道谢，可是感动得什么话也说不出来。

练习 Exercises

1. 判断正误。True or false.

(1) 马南已经工作了很多年。 (　　)

(2) 马南身上钱不多，所以不能去很好的饭馆。 (　　)

(3) 最后，付钱的是马南。 (　　)

2. 选择正确答案。Choose the correct answer.

（1）“马南的心中七上八下”的意思是（　　）。

A. 他在算钱数　B. 他很紧张　C. 他不愿意请姑妈吃饭　D. 他不高兴

（2）马南什么味道都没吃出来，是因为（　　）。

A. 他心情不好　B. 他身体不好　C. 菜的味道不好　D. 他吃得太快

（3）姑妈要去那家很讲究的饭馆，是因为（　　）。

A. 那家饭馆的菜非常好吃　B. 她知道马南想去那家饭馆

C. 她想让马南明白一个道理　D. 她太饿了就随便找了一个饭馆

小知识 Cultural Tips

面子
Face

“面子”是汉语中一个含义丰富的词汇，也是中国文化中一个深奥微妙的概念。它成为中国人日常生活和日常交际的基本概念，受到中国人异乎寻常的重视。由于中国文化强调群体本位，重视人际关系的和谐，所以中国人注重伦理关系，珍惜人情价值，而“面子”恰恰反映了中国人的这种深层文化心理。因此，中国人“爱面子”、“要面子”，做事喜欢给人“留面子”，不喜欢“驳面子”、“伤面子”，常常要“看某人的面子”、“给某人个面子”，有时甚至还得“死要面子活受罪”。

“面子” (face) in Chinese is a word of rich connotations and it is also a profound and subtle concept in the Chinese culture. As a basic concept in daily life and social interactions of Chinese people, it is extremely valued by the Chinese. Because Chinese culture emphasizes group consciousness and harmonious interpersonal relationships, it attaches great importance to ethics and values personal relationships. The mindset of “面子” reflects exactly that deep cultural mentality. Therefore, Chinese people are “sensitive about one’s reputation”, “keen on face-saving”, like to “save others’ face”, dislike “offending others’ sensitivities” or “giving offence”. They often do certain things “for the sake of somebody else ” and “do somebody a favor”. Sometimes, they “take great trouble and even suffer a lot in keeping their own face”.

22 第一笔工资

Dì yī bǐ gōngzī

My First Salary

几个不同国家的人，说着不同的语言，
他们在一起能交流吗？

打工 (dǎgōng) *v.* do manual work for others

包装 (bāozhuāng) *v.* package

运 (yùn) *v.* transport

我十六岁的时候到美国上中学。那时我第一次出去打工，工作很简单，只是把气球包装一下，然后装在箱子里运走。但是在简单的工作中我却得到了一笔丰厚的“工资”。

所有的“工人”加起来只有六个人，但是很热闹。原因很简单——我们说三种不同的语言：两个是真正的“ABC”(American Born Chinese，在美国出生的中国人)，说英语；两个是刚到美国的中国人，说汉语；还有两个是墨西哥人，当然说西班牙语了。这样的六个人到了一起会怎样呢？结果是我们居然交流得很顺畅。每个人好像都忘了对方听不懂自己的语言。两个墨西哥男孩儿好几次都用西班牙语问我事情，而另一个中国女孩儿有时也对他们说中国话。但奇怪的是，我们竟然没有一次把对方的话理解错。不光如此，我们有时还聊得很高兴，常常大声地笑起来。

这种交流不能不说是奇特的。但是静下心来想一想，也没有什么奇怪的。语言只是人们交流的工具。它帮助你了解别人，同时也让别人了解你。我们虽然使用着不同的“工具”，但是渴望交流的心情却是一样的。这使我们之间有了一种默契。我喜欢这种默契，它就是我第一次打工的“工资”，非常丰厚！

丰厚 (fēnghòu) *adj.* rich and generous

居然 (jūrán) *adv.* unexpectedly

顺畅 (shùnchàng) *adj.* smooth

奇特 (qítè) *adj.* peculiar

渴望 (kěwàng) *v.* long for, yearn for

默契 (mòqì) *n.* tacit understanding

想一想 Questions

语言点 Language Points

不光如此
besides

1. 不光如此，我们有时还聊得很高兴，常常大声地笑起来。

Besides, we sometimes chat happily and often burst into laughter.

“不光如此”，表示不只有这个，还有其他的。

“不光如此” indicates “besides”, “moreover”.

（1）手机给我们带来了很多方便。不光如此，现在的手机还有很多娱乐功能。

（2）自从去公园爬山以后，妈妈的身体好起来了。不光如此，她的心情也越来越好。

使
bring, make

2. 这使我们之间有了一种默契。

This brings tacit understanding among us.

“使”，动词。是“让”的意思，但比“让”更正式。

“使” is a verb that means “让” (let, allow), but it is more formal than “让”.

（1）北京奥运会能够使世界更加了解中国。

（2）运动可以使人身体健康、精神愉快。

练习 Exercises

1. 判断正误。True or false.

（1）我十六岁时到美国去工作。 （ ）

（2）我第一次去打工，挣了很多钱。 （ ）

（3）一起工作的六个人都说英语。 （ ）

2. 选择正确答案。Choose the correct answer.

（1）“这种交流不能不说是奇特的”，这句话的意思是（　　）。

A. 这种交流很奇怪，而且也很特别　　B. 这种交流不算奇怪，也不特别

C. 我们几个人不能交流　　D. 这种交流没有一点儿问题

（2）“我们竟然没有一次把对方的话理解错”，这句话的意思是（　　）。

A. 我们每次都理解错了　　B. 我们只有一次理解错了

C. 我们每次都理解对了　　D. 我们只有一次理解对了

（3）在“我们虽然使用着不同的‘工具’”中，“工具”指的是（　　）。

A. 机器　　B. 语言　　C. 工作　　D. 办法

小知识 Cultural Tips

剪纸艺术
The Art of Paper-Cutting

剪纸是一种古老的中国传统民间艺术。剪纸的工具和原料极其简单，而且容易找到，无论是民间剪纸艺人还是广大农村妇女，随时随地拿出剪刀和几张纸，就能发挥他们的艺术创作才能。其技艺之精，堪称巧夺天工。剪纸常常用在宗教仪式、装饰和造型艺术等方面。现在，剪纸更多的是用来装饰墙壁、门窗、房柱、镜子、灯笼等，也可以作为礼物赠送他人。

Paper-cutting is an ancient traditional folk art in China. Both the tools and materials of paper-cutting are quite simple and easy to find. Therefore, both folk artisans of paper-cutting or ordinary countrywomen can bring their artistic creativity into full play anywhere anytime with a pair of scissors and several pieces of paper. Their marvellous creations can even rival nature. Paper-cuttings are often used for religious rites, ornament and formative arts. But now, they are more widely used for decorating walls, doors, windows, mirrors and lanterns, etc. They are also good gifts for friends.

23 中国人最喜欢的运动

Zhōngguórén zuì xǐhuan de yùndòng

The Favorite Sport of the Chinese

你知道中国的“国球”是什么吗？

乒乓球 (pīngpāngqiú) *n.* table tennis

器材 (qìcái) *n.* equipment

冠军 (guànjūn) *n.* champion

盼望 (pànwàng) *v.* look forward to, expect

在中国，你知道人们最喜欢哪种运动吗？不是篮球，不是足球，而是乒乓球！

1904 年，一个上海老板从日本买回 10 套乒乓球器材，乒乓球运动从此传入中国。自从 1959 年中国运动员容国团获得第一个世界冠军后，乒乓球运动在中国发展非常快，并成为中国的“国球”。

乒乓球的重量虽然很轻，但是它在中国人心中却是很重很重的。小学生、初中生、高中生和大学生，都喜欢在课间和课后打乒乓球；其他人也经常在休息的时候打乒乓球。

每到奥运会举行的时候，中国人都盼望着看到乒乓球比赛，因为他们能够欣赏到运动员的精彩表现。如果你认为中国人只是喜欢自己国家的运动员，那你就错了。中国人也很喜欢看其他国家选手的比赛。为了观看精彩的乒乓球比赛，中国观众可以在电视机前坐上好几个小时！

现在，中国人希望有更多的外国朋友能够喜欢这个运动，希望更多的外国朋友打乒乓球，也希望大家能够一起享受这个运动的乐趣！

表现 (biǎoxiàn) *n.* performance

选手 (xuǎnshǒu) *n.* player, competitor

观看 (guānkàn) *v.* watch

观众 (guānzhòng) *n.* spectator

乐趣 (lèqù) *n.* pleasure, delight

想一想 Questions

语言点 Language Points

每到
whenever, every time

1. 每到奥运会举行的时候，中国人都盼望着看到乒乓球比赛。

Whenever the Olympic Games are being held, all the Chinese look forward to watching ping-pong matches.

"每到"，后面加表示时间的词，表示同一动作在某个时间有规律地反复出现。

"每到", with time expressions following it, means "regular recurrances of an action at a certain time".

(1) 每到春节，中国人都要和家人团聚(tuánjù：togother)。

(2) 每到周末，我都要和朋友一起去体育场踢足球。

坐上好几个小时
sit for several hours

2. 为了观看精彩的乒乓球比赛，中国观众可以在电视机前坐上好几个小时！

Chinese spectators can sit before the TV for several hours in order to follow an exciting ping-pong game.

"动词 + 上 + 数量短语"，表示动作持续的时间。

The construction of "v.+上+ numeral phrase" indicates an action lasts for a period of time.

(1) 为了买到一张足球赛的门票，人们要等上五六个小时。

(2) 每天走上半个小时，可以起到健身的作用。

练 习 Exercises

1. 判断正误。True or false.

（1）在中国，只有年轻人喜欢乒乓球运动。（　　）
（2）1959 年，乒乓球运动传入中国。（　　）
（3）中国人只喜欢看自己国家的运动员比赛。（　　）

2. 选择正确答案。Choose the correct answer.

（1）乒乓球是从（　　）传入中国的。
A. 英国　B. 韩国　C. 德国　D. 日本

（2）"乒乓球的重量虽然很轻，但是它在中国人心中却是很重很重的"，这句话的意思是（　　）。
A. 中国的乒乓球很重　B. 中国人觉得乒乓球有点儿重
C. 中国人觉得乒乓球很重要　D. 很多中国人喜欢打乒乓球

小知识 Cultural Tips

中国人的国球
National Ball Game of China

虽然乒乓球并不是中国人的发明，但长期以来中国人对这项运动有着特殊的感情。无论城乡，到处都可以见到男女老少在打乒乓球。对他们来说，这不仅是一项竞技运动，而且也是日常生活中不可缺少的健身活动。中国人在这项运动中产生了很多世界冠军，大家亲切地称他们为"国手"。20 世纪 70 年代初，中美两国乒乓球队互访成为全世界瞩目的大事，被誉为"乒乓外交"。

Although it was not invented by the Chinese people, pingpong has been the favorite sport in China for a long time. In both urban and rural areas, men and women, old and young, all play this game. For them, this is not only a competitive sport, but also an indispensable exercise in daily life. China has many world champions in this sport and people call them affectionately "national champions". This game once played an important role in the history. In the early 1970s, exchange visits by pingpong teams of China and the US became the spotlight in the world, which has since been reputed as the Pingpong Diplomacy.

24 “Sāndàjiàn” de biànhuà
“三大件”的变化

The Changes of ‘Three Important Items’

现在你通过什么来判断（pànduàn：judge）一个家庭的经济情况呢？汽车？房子？还是别的什么？如果是在30年前呢？

陌生 (mòshēng) *adj.* strange

标志 (biāozhì) *n.* mark, symbol

空调 (kōngtiáo) *n.* air conditioner

“三大件”对于今天的许多年轻人可能是个比较陌生的词汇，然而这个词却曾经是中国家庭生活水平和消费水平提高的重要标志。

在上个世纪70年代，“三大件”是手表、缝纫机、自行车，而电视这样的家用电器，对普通家庭来说还是很难想象的。到了80年代，“三大件”变成了彩电、冰箱、洗衣机。在生活还不富裕的年代，有好节目的时候，不少人会到有电视的邻居家去看电视，这样，电视就让人们聚到了一起。在90年代，“三大件”成了电话、电脑、空调。那时，一般家庭还买不起电脑，而今天电脑已经成了普通老百姓也买得起的普通电器了。这个变化仅仅用了不到20年的时间。到了21世纪的今天，“三大件”已经不再与家用电器有关，已经变成了住房、汽车和良好的子女教育。

从自行车到汽车，从电视到电脑，从解决基本穿戴问题到重视子女教育，“三大件”不断发生着新的变化。这种变化反映出几十年来中国人生活质量和生活观念的变化。

解决 (jiějué) *v.* resolve

重视 (zhòngshì) *v.* value, emphasize

不断 (bùduàn) *adv.* continuously

观念 (guānniàn) *n.* notion, thought

想一想 Questions

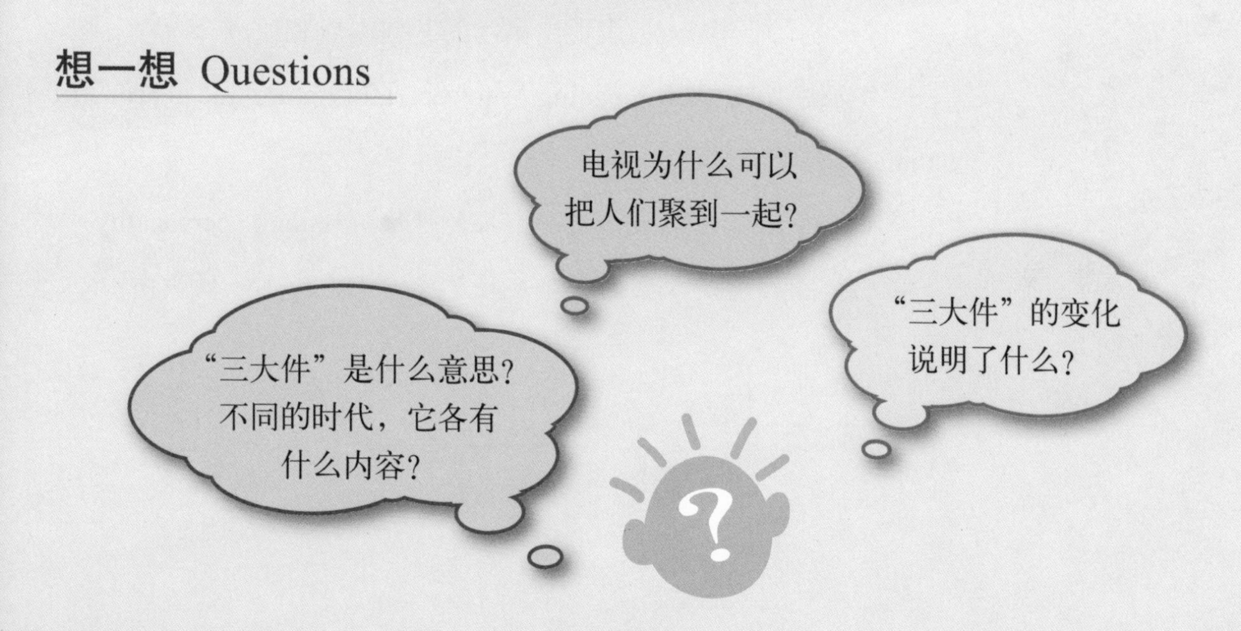

语言点 Language Points

买得（不）起
can (can't) afford

1. 而今天电脑已经成了普通老百姓也买得起的普通电器了。

Nowadays, computers have become a common electric appliance affordable to the general public.

"动词＋得（不）起"，表示有（没有）钱或能力做某事。

The construction of "v.+得（不）起" indicates someone has (not) the money or ability to do something.

（1）大排档的东西很便宜，谁都吃得起。

（2）现在手机都越来越便宜，人人都用得起。

反映
reflect

2. 这种变化反映出几十年来中国人生活质量和生活观念的变化。

This change reflects the transformation of the quality and concepts of life of the Chinese during the past several decades.

"反映"，动词。指表现出事物的某些本质和原因。

"反映" is a verb meaning "show certain nature and reasons of things".

（1）穿衣风格能反映出一个人的性格（xìnggé：personality）。

（2）出国旅游人数的增加反映了中国人生活水平的提高。

练 习 Exercises

填写下面的表格。 Fill in the table below.

	三大件的变化		
时代	三大件的内容		
20 世纪 70 年代			
20 世纪 80 年代			
20 世纪 90 年代			
21 世纪的今天			

小知识 Cultural Tips

从凭票供应到应有尽有

From Coupon-Based Supply to Abundance of Everything

今天的中国城市里，市场上各种商品琳琅满目，应有尽有。然而在几十年前，日用产品还不能满足市场需求，从食品到用品都需要凭票供应。每个中国家庭根据人口数量分配粮票、油票、布票等票证。现在可以轻易买到的自行车，在30年前却因为很难得到一张票而成为中国人心目中的奢侈品。可以说，社会经济的发展、日用产品的丰富给中国人的生活带来了翻天覆地的变化。

In Chinese cities today, there are all sorts of goods in the market. However, decades ago, the commodities of daily use in the market were in short supply. Everything from food to articles for daily use had to be purchased with coupons. Coupons for food, oil and cloth, etc., were allocated according to the number of people in each family in China. Bikes, which can be bought easily now, were once a luxury for Chinese people because a coupon for a bike was hard to obtain. Social and economic development and the abundance of commodities for daily use have transformed the life of Chinese people.

过去用的粮票
A grain coupon

25 Xià wéiqí de gùshi 下围棋的故事

A Story of Playing Go

在中国古代，如果让皇帝生气，后果（hòuguǒ：consequence）会很严重（yánzhòng：serious）。看看那些将军们是怎么做的吧。

关系 (guānxì) *n.* relationship

故意 (gùyì) *adv.* deliberately, on purpose

奖 (jiǎng) *v.* award

矛盾 (máodùn) *adj.* conflicting

明朝的皇帝朱元璋和将军徐达从小就是好朋友，关系非常好。朱元璋很喜欢下围棋，不过他的水平一般。徐达也喜欢下围棋，他的水平比朱元璋要高得多。

朱元璋经常找徐达一起下围棋。徐达是个明白人，他知道皇帝总是希望自己做什么事情都比别人好。所以每次下棋的时候，他总是故意输给皇帝，以便让皇帝高兴。

有一天，他们两个一起游玩，看到一个漂亮的湖。朱元璋突然很想下棋，就对徐达说："今天如果你能赢我，我就把这个湖奖给你。"

徐达点头同意了，但是心中很矛盾：如果自己赢了，皇帝一定会不高兴；可是如果输了，自己又舍不得这个湖。最后，他想出了一个办法，就开始认真地下棋。这次和平时不同，他丝毫也不让着皇帝，拿出所有的本领，赢了皇帝。朱元璋觉得丢了面子，正要生气，徐达说："请您看一看棋盘。"

朱元璋低头一看，发现棋盘上的棋子看起来好像"万岁"两个字。他立刻笑了，觉得徐达的水平确实很高，对他更加佩服。于是，朱元璋就把湖奖给了徐达，还为他建了一座楼，名叫"胜棋楼"。

舍不得 (shěbude) *v.* hate to part with or leave

丝毫 (sīháo) *adv.* a bit

丢面子 (diūmiànzi) lose face

万岁 (wànsuì) *v.* live long

确实 (quèshí) *adv.* indeed

佩服 (pèifú) *v.* admire

想一想 Questions

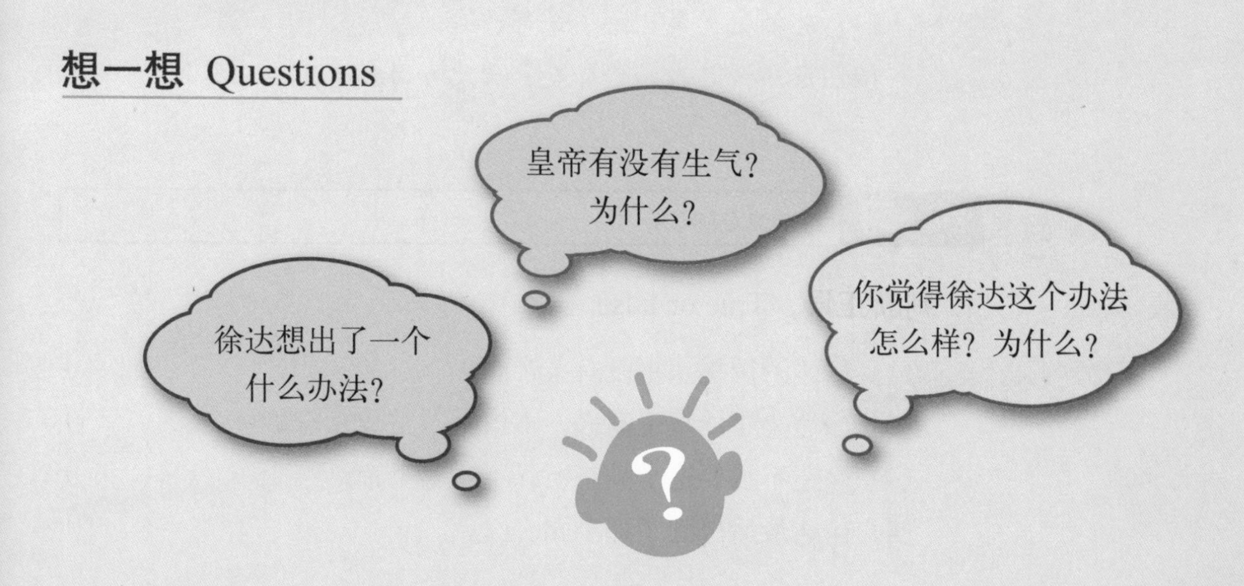

语言点 Language Points

以便
so as to

1. 他总是故意输给皇帝，以便让皇帝高兴。

He always lost the game to the emperor deliberately so as to make him happy.

“以便”，连词。表示通过前面说到的条件，让后面的事情更容易做。

“以便” is a conjunction used to show the conditions mentioned before can make the matters in question realized more easily.

(1) 这个酒店要求每个服务员会一门外语，以便更好地为顾客服务。

(2) 我要努力学好汉语，以便将来能够在中国工作。

让
give ground

2. 他丝毫也不让着皇帝。

He didn't give the slightest ground to the emperor.

“让”，动词。意思是“把好处或方便留给别人”。

“让” is a verb with the meaning “give ground to others”.

(1) 孔融把大梨让给了哥哥。

(2) 虽然他是我的好朋友，但比赛时我也不会让着他。

练习 Exercises

1. 判断正误。True or false.

(1) 徐达的围棋水平没有皇帝高。 (　　)

(2) 徐达为了让皇帝高兴，下棋时常常故意输给皇帝。 (　　)

(3) 徐达不想要这个湖，所以不想赢皇帝。 (　　)

(4) 徐达最后得到了那个湖。 (　　)

2. **请选出和划线部分意思最接近的一个。** Choose the answer closest in meaning to the underlined part.

(1) 徐达是个明白人，他知道皇帝总是希望自己做什么事情都比别人好。(   )

A. 知识很丰富的人 B. 很聪明的人

C. 有礼貌的人 D. 对别人好的人

(2) 徐达点头同意了，但是心中很矛盾。(   )

A. 心里想和皇帝打架 B. 不知怎么办才好

C. 心里很生气 D. 心里不同意

(3) 朱元璋觉得丢了面子，正要生气。(   )

A. 很丢人 B. 很惭愧 C. 很害羞 D. 很生气

小知识 Cultural Tips

皇帝与“万岁”

Emperors and ‘Wansui’ (Live Long)

皇帝是专制政治体制下一个国家的最高统治者。汉语里“皇帝”一词相传是由秦始皇创造的。秦始皇是中国历史上的第一个皇帝。在当时的社会，皇权是至高无上的，是无法被超越的权力。到了汉朝，“万岁”成为皇帝的代名词，是向皇帝表示尊敬的称呼。

The emperor is the supreme ruler in an autocratic state. The word “皇帝” in Chinese is said to be created by Emperor Qinshihuang. He was the first emperor in the history of China. His imperial power was paramount and insurmountable at that time. By Han Dynasty, “Wansui” (live long) had become the respectful synonym of the emperor.

练习答案

Answer Keys

1. √√√；DDC
2. ×√√×；CD
3. ×√√；CC
4. √×√√√×
5. ×√×；CC
6. √√√√
7. CCC
8. √×√；BC
9. ×××√；CCB
10. √×√；CC
11. √√√××
12. √√××
13. ×√；CAB
14. ××√√
15. √√√√；DB
16. ×××√
17. ××××√
18. ××√×√；DC
19. ABA
20. ××√√
21. ×√×；BAC
22. ×××；ACB
23. ×××；DC
24.

20世纪70年代	手表	缝纫机	自行车
20世纪80年代	彩电	冰箱	洗衣机
20世纪90年代	电话	电脑	空调
21世纪的今天	住房	汽车	良好的子女教育

25. ×√×√；BBA

声　明

中文天天读 *Reading China* 外研社汉语分级读物

978-7-5135-0834-6
定价：39.00

978-7-5600-8234-9
定价：39.00

978-7-5600-8235-6
定价：39.00

978-7-5600-8236-3
定价：39.00

978-7-5600-8237-0
定价：39.00

978-7-5600-9117-4
定价：42.00

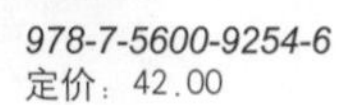

978-7-5600-9254-6
定价：42.00

978-7-5600-9159-4
定价：42.00

978-7-5135-0311-2
定价：42.00

网址： http://www.chineseplus.com **电话：** 010-88819973 **邮箱：** chinese@fltrp.com

外研社·新HSK课堂系列

MP3

978-7-5135-0427-0
定价：22.00

MP3

MP3

978-7-5600-9837-1
定价：29.00

外研社·新HSK课堂系列包含如下产品：

- “21天征服新HSK教程”系列
  《21天征服新HSK·一级教程》
  《21天征服新HSK·二级教程》
  《21天征服新HSK·三级教程》
  《21天征服新HSK·四级教程》
  《21天征服新HSK·五级教程》
  《21天征服新HSK·六级教程》

- “21天征服新HSK专项训练”系列
  《21天征服新HSK·口试》
  《21天征服新HSK·语法》
  《21天征服新HSK·写作》
  《21天征服新HSK·听力》
  《21天征服新HSK·阅读》

- “新HSK词汇”系列

- “新汉语水平考试HSK全真模拟试题”系列（含试卷、试题详解）

网址：http://www.chineseplus.com **电话**：010-88819973 **邮箱**：chinese@fltrp.com